U.S. Presidential

HISTORY

BITES

Written by Solomon Schmidt

This book is dedicated to my parents,
who have continually encouraged
and helped me throughout the
process of writing this book.

And to my great-grandpa,
for his faithful service to the Lord
and to the United States
as a World War II veteran and
Pearl Harbor survivor.

And to my great-grandma,
who passed away in 2016.
She continued to serve the Lord
and others until the end. She and my
great-grandpa were married
for almost seventy years.

A Note From the Author

U.S. Presidential History Bites is the second book in the History Bites series and was written specifically for young readers. It is full of information about the U.S. presidents and is a great resource for any American history curriculum.

It contains forty-five sections, including one about the most recent president, Donald J. Trump. To enhance comprehension, it also includes vocabulary and review questions at the end of each section, along with a glossary at the end of the book. It serves as a great read aloud but can also be enjoyed by independent readers.

My first book, U.S. History Bites, is an overview of American history, covering thirty major topics from Columbus to modern day. It also includes vocabulary and review questions at the end of each section, along with a glossary at the end of the book.

Both books were written to provide readers with bite-sized chunks of history to help them retain what they have read.

I really hope you enjoy them both.

~Solomon

TABLE OF CONTENTS

1 George Washington (1789-1797)

George Washington

Martha Washington

George Washington was born in Westmorland County, Virginia in 1732. His parents were Augustine and Mary Washington. George had seven siblings: two older brothers and five younger brothers and sisters.

When his older brother Lawrence joined the English Navy, George wanted to join, too. However, his mother would not let him because he was only eleven years old.

George grew up and became a **surveyor**. As a surveyor, he took many exciting journeys, including one in which he was almost captured by Native Americans.

During this time, the English and French controlled land in America. Each country wanted to take land from the other so they could have more power. This started a war in 1756 called the French and Indian War. George fought for the English, who eventually won.

In 1759, during the war, George married Martha Custis. She was a widowed mother of four, who became a faithful wife for George. Sadly, two of Martha's four children died young, and she and George never had any children of their own. However, she and George raised her other two children together.

After the French and Indian War, England made the American colonists pay a lot of money in **taxes**. The English did this because they had spent almost all of their money during the war and were hoping to gain some of it back by over-taxing the colonists. This made the colonists angry, and they wanted America to become an independent country, separate from England. This led to a war between the colonists and the English called the American **Revolution**, also known as the War for Independence or the Revolutionary War. The colonists chose George Washington to lead the American Continental Army, and he was a brave general during the war. Eventually, America won and became its own country.

After the war, Mr. Washington helped to form America's new **government**. He was very popular with many Americans, and in 1788, he was elected as the first United States president. He was inaugurated in New York City, which was the capital of America at that time.

President Washington established many new government positions, called the Cabinet. He also set up several new rules for the government.

One problem that President Washington helped to resolve was the Whiskey Rebellion. This rebellion started when a group of farmers got angry at the president for making them pay taxes on whiskey (alcohol). The farmers did not think that the federal government should enforce such a tax on the states, and they started marching to America's new capital (Philadelphia) to protest. However, President Washington sent soldiers to stop the angry group. By doing this, he was setting a standard that federal laws were superior to state's laws.

In 1799, two years after his presidency ended, George Washington died at his home, Mount Vernon, in Virginia.

George Washington served his country in the military and as president. He loved God, his family, and his country. Because of the leadership of President

Washington and many others, America was firmly established, and we are able to still enjoy the many freedoms we have today.

One dollar bill

The Washington Monument

Quarter

George Washington praying at Valley Forge

REVIEW BITES

VOCABULARY

Navy – A fleet of ships that fight for a country

Surveyor – Someone who measures and records the location of land and buildings

Taxes – Money that people have to pay to the government

Revolution – (This word has two meanings):
       1. A war against a government
       2. A time when things change

Government – A system that rules a country

FUN FACT

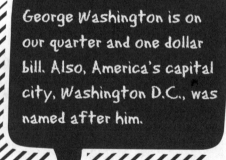

George Washington is on our quarter and one dollar bill. Also, America's capital city, Washington D.C., was named after him.

REVIEW QUESTIONS

1. What did George Washington want to join when he was eleven years old?

2. George Washington led the American Continental Army against the British during what war?

3. George Washington was elected to what position in 1788?

1.The English Navy 2. The American Revolution 3. President

2 John Adams (1797-1801)

John Adams

Abigail Adams

John Adams was born in Quincy, Massachusetts in 1735. His father was a hard-working farmer. As a young boy, John loved to play with toy boats, marbles, and kites.

John loved to learn and went to **college** at Harvard University. He graduated from there in 1755 and became a lawyer. A lawyer is a person who helps to defend someone in court. Mr. Adams worked as a lawyer in Boston for twelve years. He helped defend British soldiers in a case regarding the Boston Massacre and won despite many controversies.

In 1764, John married Abigail Smith, and they had five

children together. One of their children, John Quincy Adams, eventually became the sixth president of America.

In the early 1770s, the American **colonies** wanted to separate from England and form their own country. Mr. Adams became part of the Continental Congress, which was a group of state representatives who made decisions for the American colonies at that time.

In 1775, the American Revolution (also known as the Revolutionary War or the War for Independence) began between England and the American colonies. Mr. Adams was the one who suggested that George Washington lead the American Continental Army. Later, Mr. Adams became an **ambassador** for America during the war. He traveled to countries in Europe to get help from them for the Americans. During the war, Mr. Adams became good friends with a man named Thomas Jefferson from Virginia.

In 1783, the colonies won the American Revolution and formed their own country called the United States of America. In 1796, Americans elected John Adams to be their second president. During his presidency, he established the American Navy, and he was also the first president to live in the White House.

Around this time, Mr. Adams signed a law called the Sedition Act. This law prohibited people from saying things against the president. The reason President Adams agreed to this law was because there was a lot of arguing going on in the country regarding problems with France. Thomas Jefferson thought this law was unconstitutional because it violated Americans' freedom of speech. Eventually, by 1802, the Sedition Act (law) was repealed.

Interestingly, John Adams died on the same day as Thomas Jefferson: July 4, 1826. He was ninety years old.

Original White House

Modern White House

The Boston Massacre

One of the first U.S. Navy ships, the USS Constitution

REVIEW BITES

VOCABULARY

College – A school that people attend when they are older to learn how to do certain jobs

Colonies – Pieces of land that are ruled by another country

Ambassador – Someone who represents a country and visits other nations

FUN FACT

At this time in history, the White House was surrounded by many trees. So many that President Adams and his wife got lost one time while looking for the house.

REVIEW QUESTIONS

1. Where did John Adams go to college?

2. John Adams helped lead America during what war?

3. What law did President Adams sign that prohibited Americans from speaking out against the government?

1. Harvard University 2. The American Revolution, the War for Independence, or the Revolutionary War 3. The Sedition Act

12

Thomas Jefferson
(1801-1809)

Thomas Jefferson

Martha Jefferson

Thomas Jefferson was born in Virginia in 1734. His father owned land and worked for the government. As Thomas grew up, he studied very hard. He eventually went to the College of William and Mary and he learned a lot about science, math, and law.

Later, Thomas became an attorney, which is another name for a **lawyer**. Thomas also became a member of the Virginia House of Burgesses, which helped to rule the government of the state of Virginia.

In 1772, Thomas married Martha Skelton and they

had six children together. Sadly, Martha died before her husband became president.

During this time, the American colonies were ruled by England. The English government was over-taxing the Americans, and this made the colonists angry. So, in 1775, America went to war with England over this and many other issues. This was known as the American Revolution.

One year later, in 1776, Thomas Jefferson met with a group of American leaders to discuss things about the war. This group of men, called the Continental Congress, chose Mr. Jefferson and four other men to write a very important document called the Declaration of Independence. Mr. Jefferson wrote most of the document, and in it, he told the English government that America wanted to be its own separate country, independent (free) from England.

Mr. Jefferson did a lot to help America during the American Revolution, including **negotiating** with the French to try and get them to help America during the war. In 1783, America won the war and became its own country. Mr. Jefferson and the Continental Congress helped to set up the new American government.

Later, in 1800, Thomas Jefferson was elected as the third president of America. He helped establish the

Democratic-Republican **political party**, which believed in small government. This party no longer exists today and is not the same as the current Democratic and Republican parties. The Democratic Party we know today was established in 1828 with Andrew Jackson, and the Republican Party we know today was established in 1854 with Abraham Lincoln.

As president, one decision that Mr. Jefferson made was purchasing a lot of land from France called the Louisiana Territory. This purchase made America much larger.

Another interesting fact from this time period is that North African pirates (from Tripoli, now in modern Libya) had been attacking American merchant ships in the Mediterranean Sea. The pirates had taken American prisoners, and the pirates' leaders demanded that America pay them money (ransom) in exchange for the prisoners. Because America did not initially have a strong navy to fight the pirates, they agreed to start paying in order to get the prisoners back. Eventually, however, America refused to continue paying the pirates, and the Tripolitan War began in 1801. President Jefferson helped lead America during this time. Four years later, in 1805, a peace treaty was signed, the prisoners were ransomed (paid for and released), and the fighting ended with neither side winning.

In 1809, after President Jefferson's terms had ended, he moved back to his Virginia home, Monticello. He enjoyed playing the violin and collecting thousands of books. Mr. Jefferson also started a college called the University of Virginia. Shortly after this, he died on July 4, 1826, the same day John Adams died.

Nickel

Two dollar bill

Declaration of Independence

The Louisiana Purchase

The Jefferson Memorial

REVIEW BITES

VOCABULARY

Lawyer – Another word for attorney; a person who practices law

Negotiating – Trying to arrive at agreements with other people or countries

Political Party – A group of people who believe certain things about how the government should run

FUN FACT

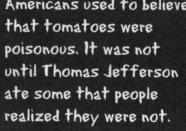

Americans used to believe that tomatoes were poisonous. It was not until Thomas Jefferson ate some that people realized they were not.

REVIEW QUESTIONS

1. Thomas Jefferson was part of what group that helped to rule Virginia?

2. What important document did Thomas Jefferson mainly write?

3. What was the name of Thomas Jefferson's home in Virginia?

1. The House of Burgesses 2. The Declaration of Independence
3. Monticello

18

4 James Madison (1809-1817)

James Madison

Dolley Madison

James Madison was born in Port Conaway, Virginia in 1751. His parents were James and Eleanor and they lived on an **estate** called Montpelier. James completed school when he was eighteen years old and went on to attend Princeton University.

During the American Revolution, Mr. Madison worked as part of the Continental Congress. This was a group of state representatives, who led the American colonies at that time. Mr. Madison helped to make many important decisions for America during this time.

After America won the American Revolution against the English, Mr. Madison helped to write the United States **Constitution** and the Bill of Rights. The Bill of Rights describes all of the rights and freedoms that Americans have. Since Mr. Madison contributed so much to the U.S. Constitution, he is known as the "Father of the Constitution."

In 1794, James Madison married a **widow** named Dolley Todd. Dolley had grown up as a Quaker. The Quakers were a religious group of people who believed in simple ways of living and worship, and they were devoted to peaceful principles. James and Dolley Madison became popular among many Americans because of their kindness and compassion.

In 1800, when Thomas Jefferson was elected president, Mr. Madison was appointed as his secretary of state. This job involves a lot of important decision-making regarding America's relationships with other countries.

In 1808, James Madison was elected as the fourth president of America. During his presidency, the War of 1812 broke out between the Americans and the English. The English had been mistreating American **sailors** by capturing them and forcing them to join the

English Navy. During this war, the English also came into Washington, D.C. and burned down the White House in retaliation (revenge) for the American attack on the city of York in Ontario, Canada. Thankfully, Dolley Madison saved a famous portrait of George Washington along with important government documents before the English came. After the English left Washington, D.C., the Americans returned to the city and rebuilt the White House and other buildings that had also been destroyed.

In 1814, the War of 1812 ended. Both sides had come to an agreement to end the fighting. America had won many of the battles on land and sea. This was important for President Madison because he showed the rest of the world that America could fight a war on its own without help from other countries. However, in order to help pay for the war, President Madison raised taxes to an all-time high.

In 1817, James Madison's presidency ended, and he went back to his home, Montpelier, in Virginia. Before he died, Mr. Madison helped Thomas Jefferson establish the University of Virginia. James Madison died on June 28, 1836 at the age of eighty-five.

English soldiers burning the White House during the War of 1812

Five thousand dollar bill

The United States Constitution

REVIEW BITES

VOCABULARY

Estate – A big piece of land with a large house

Constitution – A document that explains a country's laws

Widow – A woman whose husband has died

Sailors – Men and women who work on ships in a country's navy

FUN FACT

James Madison was the smallest president. He was 5 feet 4 inches tall and only weighed one hundred pounds. Someone once said that he was "no bigger than a bar of soap."

REVIEW QUESTIONS

1. What were the two important documents that James Madison helped to create?

2. Whom did James Madison marry?

3. What did the English do to the White House during the War of 1812?

1.The U.S. Constitution and the Bill of Rights 2. Dolley Todd 3. Burned it

5

James Monroe
(1817-1825)

James Monroe

Elizabeth Monroe

James Monroe was born in Westmorland County, Virginia in 1758. Like other presidents before him, James grew up on a farm in Virginia. His father was a carpenter, who owned a large piece of land, and James loved to hunt and go horseback riding. Growing up, James was homeschooled for many years until he went to a school called Campbelltown Academy.

In 1774, after James' parents died, he attended the College of William and Mary. In 1776, when the American Revolution started, James joined the war and was a very brave soldier. He fought together with General George Washington in the Battle of Trenton. At the end of his time as a soldier, James decided to go into politics.

In 1786, Mr. Monroe married Elizabeth Kortright, and they had three children together.

At the beginning of his political **career**, Mr. Monroe became a United States **Senator** and worked in the U.S. Senate for several years. After that, he was elected as the governor of Virginia. During Thomas Jefferson's presidency, Mr. Monroe worked together with him to help make a deal with France called the Louisiana Purchase. This purchase gave America a lot more land and made the country larger (see map on page 16). While James Madison was president, Mr. Monroe worked as his secretary of war during the War of 1812.

In 1816, James Monroe ran for president and won. He was a Democratic-Republican, just like James Madison and Thomas Jefferson before him.

While Mr. Monroe was president for eight years, he did a lot of work on **foreign policy**. In one instance, he helped negotiate the purchase of Florida from Spain. He also came up with something called the Monroe Doctrine. This was a document that told countries in Europe that they could not establish any more **colonies** in America. The Monroe Doctrine was extremely important because it helped to protect America's independence.

Also, during his first term as president, the country experienced a hard time called the Panic of 1819. During this time, many people lost a lot of money because of financial problems with the banks. Despite these hardships, the time while James Monroe was president is known as "The Era of Good Feelings" because many Americans felt good about the way the country was running overall.

In 1825, when his presidency ended, James Monroe went back home to Virginia. He spent some of his time speaking out against the issue of slavery. Mr. Monroe thought that the slaves were being treated unfairly, and he argued that slavery should stop. (Slavery was when black people were owned by white people and were made to do work for them.)

In 1830, Mr. Monroe's wife, Elizabeth, died, and he was deeply saddened. He only lived for ten more months and died that same year at age seventy-three.

General George Washington crossing the Delaware River with
James Monroe standing behind him

The Panic of 1819

President Monroe and advisors creating the Monroe Doctrine

REVIEW BITES

VOCABULARY

Career – A job someone keeps for a long time

Senator – A person who works in a part of the government called the U.S. Senate

Foreign policy – The decisions a government makes about how they are going to deal with other countries

Colonies – Pieces of land that are ruled by another country

FUN FACT

In 1821, President Monroe ran unopposed for a second term. He won every electoral vote, except for one. William Plumer of New Hampshire purposely did not vote for him so that George Washington would be the only president to have been elected unanimously.

REVIEW QUESTIONS

1. James Monroe fought alongside George Washington during what war?

2. What deal did James Monroe make with the French while Thomas Jefferson was president?

3. What important doctrine did James Monroe create while he was president?

1. The American Revolution 2. The Louisiana Purchase 3. The Monroe Doctrine

6

John Quincy Adams
(1825-1829)

John Quincy Adams

Louisa Adams

John Quincy Adams was born in Massachusetts on July 11, 1767. He was the son of America's second president, John Adams.

John was just a boy during the American Revolution. When he was only eight years old, he stood on a hilltop with his mother and watched the Battle of Bunker Hill, which took place in Boston, Massachusetts.

When John was a teenager, he and his father traveled to the Netherlands during the American Revolution. They went there to **negotiate** with the Dutch people to see if they would help America during the war.

While there, John Quincy studied many things and enjoyed music, art, and fencing. Around that same time, a man named Francis Dana asked John to go to Russia with him to be his personal secretary.

After his time in Europe, John Quincy returned to America where he studied at Harvard University. He then started to write editorials for newspapers, called the "Letters of Publicola," and said that George Washington was doing a great job as president. Because of this and other reasons, President Washington decided to make Mr. Adams an **ambassador** to the Netherlands in 1794.

Three years later, in 1797, Mr. Adams married an English woman named Louisa Johnson, and they had four children together. Louisa Adams loved to write poems and kept many journals.

Mr. Adams then went on to work for his father, President John Adams and also for Presidents Jefferson, Madison, and Monroe. While James Monroe was president, Mr. Adams helped him write the Monroe Doctrine, which protected America from European countries trying to colonize them again.

In 1824, Mr. Adams ran for president against

Andrew Jackson. After a difficult campaign, Mr. Adams won and became America's sixth president.

President Adams was not able to accomplish a lot during his term because Andrew Jackson and his supporters would try to stop everything the president wanted to do. However, one thing President Adams was able to accomplish was building an important canal system, which connected the Chesapeake Bay and the Ohio River. Also, in 1828, during his presidency, the Baltimore and Ohio Railroad was built.

Since Andrew Jackson had created such a stir and had become so popular with many Americans, he won the next presidential election, defeating President Adams.

After his presidency, Mr. Adams became a U.S. Representative for eighteen years. While serving in that role, Mr. Adams spoke out against slavery and some of the things Andrew Jackson was doing as president.

In 1848, Mr. Adams suffered a stroke while in the U.S. House of Representatives. He died on February 23, 1848, in Washington, D.C. at the age of eighty.

Battle of Bunker Hill during the American Revolution

John Quincy Adams collapsing after
suffering a stroke in the
U.S. House of Representatives

REVIEW BITES

VOCABULARY

Negotiate – To try to arrive at agreements with people or countries

Ambassador – Someone who represents a country and visits other nations

Campaign (noun) – An organized effort to get someone elected to a political position

Supporters – People who like a person and agree with his or her decisions

Representative – A person who works in a part of the federal government called the House of Representatives

FUN FACT

One time while President John Quincy Adams was swimming in the Potomac River, someone stole his clothes. He asked a boy who was walking by to get him some new clothes from the White House.

REVIEW QUESTIONS

1. Where did John Quincy Adams live and work as Francis Dana's personal secretary?

2. John Quincy Adams served as a U.S. ambassador to which country?

3. What railroad was built during John Quincy Adams' presidency?

1. Russia 2. The Netherlands 3. The Baltimore and Ohio Railroad

Andrew Jackson

Rachel Jackson

Andrew Jackson was born in a log cabin in South Carolina in 1767. Andrew was called the "People's President" because he was the first president who grew up like an ordinary American. Andrew was known for his hot temper (anger) and bravery. Although he only attended school occasionally, Andrew eventually became a good public speaker.

In 1780, at only thirteen years old, Andrew joined the American Continental Army during the American Revolution. One time, he was captured by the English and kept as a prisoner. While he was a prisoner, Andrew was once told to clean an English soldier's boots. He said, "no," and the English soldier cut him on the forehead with his sword.

After the American Revolution, Mr. Jackson became an **attorney**. In 1791, he married a woman named Rachel Donelson. Although they never had any biological children, they did have two adopted sons. Sadly, Mrs. Jackson died shortly before her husband became president.

When the War of 1812 began against the English, Mr. Jackson joined the fighting. He eventually became a general because of his bravery and victories. He won many battles, including the Battle of New Orleans. During that battle, General Jackson and his soldiers killed and captured many English soldiers. This battle made Mr. Jackson popular with many Americans.

In 1821, Mr. Jackson became the first military **governor** of Florida. This meant that he was a military officer given governmental control over the territory. One year later, in 1822, Mr. Jackson became a U.S. Senator.

In 1824, Mr. Jackson ran for president but lost to

John Quincy Adams. However, he ran again in 1828 and this time, he defeated President Adams and was elected as the seventh American president. He was the first person from the newly established Democratic Party to become president. There was a huge celebration for his victory, but because it was so noisy, President Jackson ended up leaving to stay the night in a hotel.

During this same time in history, the Native Americans (then referred to as Indians) lived all over the Eastern United States. President Jackson did not like this, so, in 1830, he made a law that forced the Native Americans to leave their homes in the East and move out west. This law was called the Indian Removal Act.

Also, while he was president, Mr. Jackson decided to get rid of the **National Bank** and lowered America's **debt** more than any other president. Ironically, however, during his retirement, Mr. Jackson ended up having to borrow money because the country suffered economically due to his closing the National Bank a few years before. These financially difficult times are known as the Panic of 1837 (see section 8).

As a side note: President Jackson was known for his fiery temper and aggressive personality. One time, during his presidency, Mr. Jackson was almost killed by a man who shot a gun at him. However, the gun misfired, and President Jackson ran after the man with a cane.

After his presidency ended, Mr. Jackson went back to his home, the Hermitage, in Tennessee. In 1845, he died from tuberculosis and heart failure at the age of seventy-eight.

Twenty dollar bill

Battle of New Orleans

REVIEW BITES

VOCABULARY

Attorney – Another word for lawyer; a person who practices law

Governor – Someone who leads a state or territory

National Bank – The system of banking and money for a whole country

Debt – Money that people or a country owe to someone else

FUN FACT

While Andrew Jackson was fighting in the Creek Indian War, one man who served under him was David Crockett. David (Davy) Crockett became a famous American frontiersman.

REVIEW QUESTIONS

1. What happened to Andrew Jackson during the American Revolution?

2. What political party was established with Andrew Jackson as their first president?

3. What did Andrew Jackson eliminate while he was president?

1. He was captured by the English
2. The Democratic Party 3. The National Bank

Martin Van Buren
(1837-1841)

Martin Van Buren

Hannah Van Buren

Martin Van Buren was born in Kinderhook, New York in 1837. Martin's father was a farmer and owned an inn where many politicians came to stay.

When he was thirteen years old, Martin quit school and began working at a law office. Around this time, many people began to notice that he was a very good speaker.

At just eighteen years old, Martin helped Thomas Jefferson get elected as America's third president. This made Martin more well known throughout the country.

In 1807, Martin married Hannah Hoes. Sadly, she died

before her husband became president, and Martin had to raise their four sons by himself.

In 1812, five years after he married Hannah, Mr. Van Buren became a U.S. Senator in New York. He founded a political group called the Albany Regency and attended New York's second **Constitutional Convention.**

In 1828, Mr. Van Buren was elected as the governor of New York. While he was governor, he helped to get Andrew Jackson elected as America's seventh president.

While Andrew Jackson was president, Mr. Van Buren worked as his secretary of state. This is a very important job that involves a lot of decision-making regarding America's relationships with other countries. When President Jackson ran a second time, he chose Mr. Van Buren to be his vice presidential candidate. Together, they won, and Mr. Van Buren became the next vice president of America.

In 1836, near the end of Andrew Jackson's presidency, Mr. Van Buren ran for president as a Democrat and won. One of the reasons Mr. Van Buren won was because he told the American people that he would make decisions similar to that of President Jackson, and this pleased many Americans.

One year later, a **depression** called the Panic of 1837 began. Many businesses and banks failed, which made them lose all of their money. President Van Buren tried to help by making a stronger **banking system** for America. Unfortunately, President Van Buren continued living lavishly, buying many things for himself. This made many Americans angry because he was getting richer while they were getting poorer.

One time, while Mr. Van Buren was president, America and Canada almost fought in a war because they could not decide on **borders** between their countries. President Van Buren helped to prevent a war by negotiating a peace deal with Canada that eventually led to the Webster-Ashburton Treaty in 1842.

Just like Andrew Jackson, President Van Buren also forced Native Americans (Indians) to move out west. In 1838, the Cherokee Indians were forced to take a long and difficult journey to what is now the state of Oklahoma. As a result, many of them suffered and died. This is why their journey is known as the "Trail of Tears."

Because of the problems that occurred while Martin Van Buren was president, he did not get reelected in 1841. After his presidency ended, Martin Van Buren went home to Kinderhook, New York, where he died on July 24, 1862, during the time of the Civil War (also known as the War Between the States). He was seventy-nine years old.

"O.K." political cartoon
(see "Fun Fact" on next page)

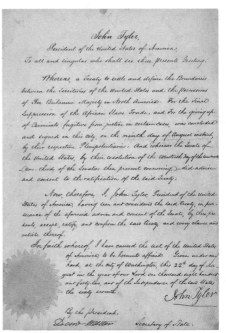

Webster-Ashburton Treaty

The Trail of Tears

REVIEW BITES

VOCABULARY

Constitutional Convention – A place where many important people meet to discuss America's Constitution

Depression – A time when businesses stop running and many people lose their jobs

Banking System – A system of banks that takes care of a country's money

Borders – Lines of separation between countries

FUN FACT

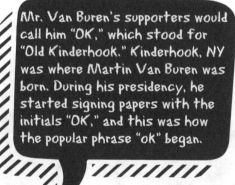

Mr. Van Buren's supporters would call him "OK," which stood for "Old Kinderhook." Kinderhook, NY was where Martin Van Buren was born. During his presidency, he started signing papers with the initials "OK," and this was how the popular phrase "ok" began.

REVIEW QUESTIONS

1. For whom did Martin Van Buren serve as vice president?

2. What was the long and difficult journey of the Cherokee Indians called?

3. What was the economic depression called during Martin Van Buren's presidency?

9

William Henry Harrison
(1841)

William Henry Harrison

Anna Harrison

William Henry Harrison was born in Virginia in 1773. William's father, Benjamin, was a member of the Continental Congress, a group of state representatives who made decisions for the American colonies at that time. His father was also one of the signers of the Declaration of Independence. William grew up knowing George Washington and other important Americans because they were friends with his father.

After finishing school, William attended Hampden-Sydney College to study medicine, history, and literature.

Soon after completing college, William decided to join the military forces and became a part of the First Infantry of the Regular Army. William fought for four years in a war against the Native Americans called the Northwest Indian War. One of the major battles in which he fought was called the Battle of Fallen Timbers. William also became an assistant to a popular general named Anthony Wayne.

In 1795, during his time in the military, Mr. Harrison married a woman named Anna Symmes. They had nine children together.

After Mr. Harrison fought in the Northwest Indian War, President John Adams made him secretary for the new Northwest **Territory**. Mr. Harrison proposed "The Harrison Land Act of 1800," which made it easier for Americans to purchase land in this area of the country.

During the War of 1812, Mr. Harrison led many important battles. The most famous battle he led was the Battle of Tippecanoe, in which he and his soldiers defeated a Native American leader named Tecumseh. Because of this battle, Mr. Harrison became known as "Old Tippecanoe."

Once the War of 1812 ended, Mr. Harrison was elected as a U.S. Senator and then as a U.S.

Representative a few years later. In 1836, he ran for president but lost to Martin Van Buren. He ran again in 1841 under the Whig **political party** and won.

While campaigning for president, Mr. Harrison became the first candidate to have a campaign slogan, or saying. His slogan was "Tippecanoe and Tyler, Too." "Tippecanoe" was talking about Mr. Harrison, and "Tyler" was talking about his vice presidential running mate, John Tyler.

At his presidential inauguration, Mr. Harrison gave a very long speech. It was pouring rain, and he did not wear a coat to protect himself from the cold. He ended up catching **pneumonia** and died one month later in 1841. William Henry Harrison served the shortest time as president. Vice President John Tyler then became the next president.

No one knows what Mr. Harrison might have accomplished while he was president. We do know that he believed in small government, meaning that he did not want the government to be too powerful over the people. We also know that he was in favor of slavery.

General Anthony Wayne

Battle of Tippecanoe

The Northwest Territory (in dark yellow)

REVIEW BITES

VOCABULARY

Literature – Writings by old or famous authors

Territory – A piece of land that is not a state

Political Party – A group of people who believe certain things about how government should run

Pneumonia – A sickness in your lungs that affects your breathing

FUN FACT

William Henry Harrison had many children and grandchildren. One of his grandchildren was Benjamin Harrison, who became America's twenty-third president (see section 23).

REVIEW QUESTIONS

1. Against whom did William Henry Harrison fight while he was in the U.S. Army?

2. What battle made William Henry Harrison famous?

3. How long did William Henry Harrison serve as president?

10

John Tyler
(1841-1845)

John Tyler

Julia Tyler

John Tyler was born in Virginia on March 29, 1790. He grew up on his family's land in Virginia called Greenway Plantation. Sadly, when John was only seven years old, his mother died. His father then had to take care of John and his seven brothers and sisters alone.

Until the age of twelve, John went to school in Virginia. After that, he went to a preparatory school for the College of William and Mary. In his spare time, he enjoyed playing the violin and writing poetry. In 1807, John finished college and became a lawyer.

Six years later, in 1813, Mr. Tyler married Letitia Christian. Sadly, Mrs. Tyler died while her husband was president. Mr. Tyler eventually married another woman named Julia Gardiner. Interestingly, Mr. Tyler had the most children of any president: fifteen in all. He had eight children with his first wife and seven with his second.

In 1811, Mr. Tyler was elected into Virginia's **legislature**. In 1816, he was elected into the U.S. House of Representatives, and in 1825, he became the governor of Virginia. In 1826, he was elected into the U.S. Senate. (As a side note: the U.S. Senate and House of Representatives together are called Congress. These two "houses" make America's laws.)

In 1841, Mr. Tyler became William Henry Harrison's vice president. When President Harrison died one month after his inauguration, Mr. Tyler immediately became the next president.

Because his father had been a **judge**, Mr. Tyler knew the Constitution very well and tried hard to follow it. Although many people thought he did not have the right to become president, Mr. Tyler knew that the **Constitution** clearly stated that the vice president assumes the role of president if it is vacated for any reason. However, the Constitution did not say how long the vice president is to remain the president. While Congress tried to resolve this issue, Mr. Tyler decided to take the oath of office and become president without Congress' approval. This settled the issue and set the guidelines for all future vice presidents.

While he was president, Mr. Tyler made many enemies. Government workers and politicians got angry with President Tyler because he vetoed many laws. When a president vetoes a bill, it means he refuses to sign it into law. President Tyler even vetoed laws that some of his friends wanted. Because of this, many people tried to impeach him but failed.

During his presidency, Mr. Tyler helped prevent a war from happening between America, Great Britain, and Canada. He also helped to make Texas a part of America in 1845 and began trading goods and supplies with China.

In 1845, Mr. Tyler's presidency ended, and he went back home to Virginia.

Later, in 1861, when the Civil War began, Mr. Tyler worked to help the state of Virginia separate from the United States of America (which is called seceding from the Union). He was elected into the Confederate Congress, which was the government of the states that separated from America. Because Mr. Tyler joined the Confederate Congress, some people thought that he was a traitor (someone who betrays their country). However, before he could begin his work in the Confederate Congress, Mr. Tyler died in Virginia in January of 1862, during the Civil War. He was seventy-one years old.

Texas Territory

Confederate Congress

REVIEW BITES

VOCABULARY

Plantation – A large farm or estate with resident workers

Legislature – A form of government, usually in a city or state

Judge – Someone who makes decisions in a court based on the law

Constitution – A document that explains a country's laws

Impeach – To remove a public official from his/her office

FUN FACT

People who did not agree that John Tyler was president sent him mail labeled "Acting President." He would not even read the letters and would just send them back to the people unopened.

59

REVIEW QUESTIONS

1. John Tyler worked in which state's government?

2. Why did John Tyler make enemies while he was president?

3. After he was president, what did John Tyler help Virginia to do?

1. Virginia 2. Because he vetoed many laws, some that even his friends wanted 3. Separate from the United States of America/secede from the Union

11

James K. Polk
(1845-1849)

James K. Polk

Sarah Polk

James Polk was born in North Carolina in 1795. As a child, he had many health problems, which prevented him from going to school until he was seventeen years old. Eventually, he was diagnosed with gall stones and needed surgery to remove them. Thankfully, he began to get better and went to school.

While at school, James studied Greek and Latin and learned how to read. After finishing school, he went to the University of North Carolina. At first, he wanted to be a lawyer but eventually went into **politics** instead.

In 1824, James married Sarah Childress. They never had any children. Mrs. Polk learned about being a **first lady** from Dolley Madison, James Madison's wife.

In 1825, Mr. Polk was elected as a U.S. Representative. He later became the Speaker of the U.S. House of Representatives, where he worked for ten years. In 1839, he was elected as the governor of Tennessee.

Later, in 1844, the Democrats chose Mr. Polk to be their candidate for president. While he ran for president, Mr. Polk promised to do many things that the American people liked. Because of this, he was elected president but only won by a small margin (little bit).

During his presidency, Mr. Polk reestablished the Independent Treasury System because he did not want the federal government to have exclusive banking power. Also, during that time, America was trading goods with other countries, but America's tariffs were so high that some countries did not want to trade with them. The tariffs were taxes that countries had to pay in order to trade with America. President Polk worked to lower the tariffs so that countries would want to trade more with America.

President Polk also worked peacefully with Great Britain to decide where the border between America and Canada would be located. It was eventually decided to be the 49th Parallel.

Also, during Mr. Polk's time as president, Mexico and America fought a war from 1846 to 1848 called the Mexican-American War. The two countries fought over who would get more land in Texas. America won easily, and because of the war, President Polk purchased a lot of land from Mexico. America then became much larger because it bought all the land that eventually became the states of New Mexico, Colorado, Wyoming, Arizona, Utah, Nevada, and California. However, this cost America a lot of money, and it made America's **debt** much larger.

An interesting side note is that James Polk was called "Young Hickory." He believed in many of the same things as Andrew Jackson, and Andrew Jackson was called "Old Hickory."

In 1849, after his presidency ended, Mr. Polk went back home to Tennessee. Three months later, he died on June 15, 1849, in Tennessee at age fifty-three.

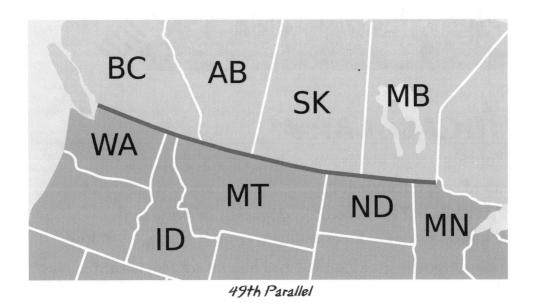

49th Parallel

The Mexican-American War

REVIEW BITES

VOCABULARY

Politics – The involvement in a city's, state's, or country's government

First lady – The wife of a governor or president

Representative – A person who works in a part of the federal government called the House of Representatives

Debt – Money that people or a country owe to someone else

FUN FACT

Sarah Polk did not allow people to dance or drink wine in the White House. One time, during a party to celebrate her husband becoming president, Mrs. Polk made everyone stop dancing.

REVIEW QUESTIONS

1. What border was established during James Polk's presidency?

2. What did President Polk lower so that other countries would trade with America?

3. As a result of winning the Mexican-American War, what did America gain?

1. Between America and Canada (the 49th Parallel)   2. Tariffs
3. More land that made Texas bigger, along with land that eventually became New Mexico, Colorado, Wyoming, Arizona, Utah, Nevada, and California

12

Zachary Taylor
(1849-1850)

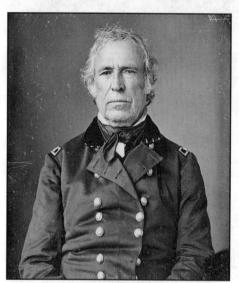

Zachary Taylor

Margaret Taylor

Zachary Taylor was born in Orange County, Virginia in 1784. Zachary did not go to school very much because his father did not make him. However, he did eventually attend the College of William and Mary where many other presidents before him had gone. Interestingly, one of Zachary's cousins was James Madison.

In 1806, he joined the Kentucky **militia** and began his forty-year career as a soldier, eventually becoming a brigadier general. One time during the War of 1812, Mr. Taylor held off four hundred Native Americans with only fifty soldiers. After the war, Mr. Taylor helped to settle land disputes between the Native Americans and new American settlers.

Earlier, in 1810, Mr. Taylor met Margaret Smith and they were married soon after. They had six children together. Sadly, two of their daughters died from a bad fever. As a result, Mrs. Taylor also became sick and was unhealthy for the rest of her life. Interestingly, she did not want to serve as first lady, so one of her daughters did instead.

Mr. Taylor also fought in two other wars against the Native Americans: the Black Hawk War and the Second Seminole War. During these wars, he won many battles and attained a high position in the military.

During the Mexican-American War (see section 11), General Taylor won every battle he fought, which helped America win the war. Because of his bravery in battle, he was called "Old Rough and Ready."

In 1849, Mr. Taylor was elected as America's twelfth president. While president, he gave the California and New Mexico territories the option of becoming states, but they did not join during his presidency.

Also, during this time, some of the new states

wanted to allow slavery while others did not. President Taylor helped to calm the **tensions**, and when some states wanted to separate (secede) from America, President Taylor said that he would send the U.S. Army to stop them. Because of this, those states did not secede, and the country did not divide while Mr. Taylor was president.

In 1850, on a hot summer day, President Taylor decided to drink some ice cold milk with a bowl of cherries. Shortly after doing that, President Taylor became very ill, and some people believed that this snack may have given him indigestion, gastroenteritis, or cholera. Because of the sickness, President Taylor died on July 9, 1850. He had only been president for one year and was the second president to die **in office**. Vice President Millard Fillmore then became the next president.

Although President Taylor was not able to accomplish many things, he did stop some of the states from separating from the Union. This helped to prevent the states from going to war against each other.

Zachary Taylor commanding troops during the Mexican-American War

United States map, including the California and New Mexico territories

REVIEW BITES

VOCABULARY

Militia – A separate group of soldiers formed from each state, not part of the military

Tensions – Problems

In office – Serving in a political job, like the presidency

FUN FACT

Many people said that Zachary Taylor was a humble man, even when he fought in battle. Instead of wearing a fancy uniform, General Taylor sometimes wore old farm clothes and a straw hat.

REVIEW QUESTIONS

1. How long did Zachary Taylor serve in the military?

2. What was Zachary Taylor's nickname while he was in the military?

3. What did Zachary Taylor prevent America from doing while he was president?

1. Forty years 2. "Old Rough and Ready" 3. Separating because of slavery

13 Millard Fillmore (1850-1853)

Millard Fillmore

Abigail Fillmore

Millard Fillmore was born in Locke, New York in 1800. He became America's thirteenth president after President Zachary Taylor died.

Millard grew up with almost no schooling because his parents were so poor. He had to work very hard to help himself and his family. Millard taught himself how to read and used the Bible as his primary reading book.

When he was nineteen years old, Millard entered a school called Hope Academy. While there, he got to know his teacher, Abigail Powers. Seven years later, in 1826, they got married and had two children together. While her husband was president, Mrs. Fillmore set up a White House Library. She also did not allow people to smoke or drink alcohol in the White House, just like Sarah Polk.

After finishing school, Mr. Fillmore decided that he wanted to be a **lawyer**. He studied law on his own, worked for a local attorney, and studied hard using the law office's free library books. However, he eventually changed his mind and decided to pursue a career in politics instead.

In 1829, Mr. Fillmore was elected as an **assemblyman** in New York. He was elected three times to that position. He was then elected into the U.S. House of Representatives in Washington, D.C. Mr. Fillmore became an important political leader as a Representative.

In 1844, he tried to become the governor of New York but was unsuccessful. Four years later, a **political party** called the Whigs chose Mr. Fillmore to be Zachary Taylor's vice presidential candidate. Zachary Taylor won the presidential election, and Mr. Fillmore became the vice president of America. In 1850, Zachary Taylor died, making Millard Fillmore the next president.

As president, Mr. Fillmore signed the **Compromise** of 1850. This law was meant to please both the South and the North on the issue of slavery. With this law,

California became a state that did not allow slavery. This law also allowed government soldiers to help capture runaway slaves who had escaped to the North. This made President Fillmore very unpopular with his political party, the Whigs, because they wanted slavery to be abolished.

In 1853, President Fillmore sent a man named Matthew Perry to Japan. For two hundred years, Japan had not traded with any other countries. So, President Fillmore had Matthew Perry make an agreement with the Japanese to start trading with America. The Japanese agreed and eventually started trading in 1854.

Because of the controversy surrounding the Compromise of 1850, the Whigs did not choose President Fillmore as their candidate for the next presidential election. So, after his term ended in 1853, Mr. Fillmore went back home to New York. Interestingly, he decided to run for president again in 1856 but came in third place.

While living in Buffalo, New York, Mr. Fillmore helped to create many important organizations. These included the Buffalo General Hospital, the Buffalo Fine Arts Academy, the Buffalo Historic Society, and the Buffalo chapter for the Society for the Prevention of Cruelty to Animals (SPCA). He was also the first chancellor of the University of Buffalo. There is also a hospital in Buffalo,

New York named after him, called Millard Fillmore Suburban Hospital.

Millard Fillmore died in Buffalo in 1874 after suffering from a stroke. He was seventy-four years old.

Matthew Perry

Millard Fillmore Suburban Hospital

State University of New York at Buffalo

REVIEW BITES

VOCABULARY

Lawyer – Another word for attorney; a person who practices law

Assemblyman – A man who works in part of a state's government called the Assembly

Political Party – A group of people who believe certain things about how the government should run

Compromise – An agreement that pleases people on both sides of an argument

FUN FACT

While Millard Fillmore was president, the first bathtub was built in the White House.

REVIEW QUESTIONS

1. While learning how to read, what was Millard Fillmore's primary reading book?

2. Millard Fillmore was elected to government offices from which state?

3. While he was president, what major law did Millard Fillmore sign that helped to solve issues about slavery?

1. The Bible 2. New York 3. The Compromise of 1850

14 Franklin Pierce (1853-1857)

Franklin Pierce

Jane Pierce

Franklin Pierce was born in a log cabin in New Hampshire on November 23, 1804. He had seven brothers and sisters.

Franklin went to school for a few years and eventually attended Bowdoin **College** where he worked with two men named Henry Wadsworth Longfellow and Nathaniel Hawthorne. These men became very famous American authors. At first, Franklin did not do well in college, but he eventually worked harder and became a much better student.

From 1833 to 1837, Mr. Pierce served in the U.S. Congress, which is made up of the Senate and the House of Representatives. He was also elected into important political positions in the state of New Hampshire.

In 1834, Mr. Pierce married Jane Appleton. They had three children together, but sadly, they all died young. This made Mrs. Pierce very sad. She was a very shy and mentally unstable woman to begin with and hated politics and Washington, D.C. She never wanted her husband to become president. Because of these things, Mrs. Pierce did not function well as first lady and often relied on her aunt to help her with her duties.

When the Mexican-American War started in 1846 (see section II), Mr. Pierce joined the U.S. Army. One time, he fainted during a battle, and when he returned home from the war, people made fun of him for it and called him a **coward**.

In 1852, the Democrats chose Mr. Pierce as their candidate to run for president. He won by a large margin, mainly because the Democrats were very popular at that time. So, in 1853, Franklin Pierce became the fourteenth president of the United States.

One important thing that President Pierce

accomplished was the Gadsden Purchase. This allowed America to buy the southern parts of Arizona and New Mexico from Mexico, giving the continental U.S. the full shape that it is today.

In 1854, President Pierce signed the Kansas-Nebraska Act. This law ended the Missouri Compromise of 1820 and allowed slavery to spread north of Missouri. It gave Kansas and Nebraska the right to choose whether or not they would allow slavery. This angered many people in these two states, which led to a lot of fighting. Because the violent conflicts caused many injuries and even several deaths, Kansas was called "Bleeding Kansas." At this time, the rest of America became even more divided over the issue of slavery.

Sadly, President Pierce had a bad habit of drinking too much alcohol and got drunk on several occasions. He thought that drinking would help him forget his problems and sadness, but it only made things worse.

In 1857, President Pierce's term ended. The Democratic Party did not renominate him for a second term because they were so embarrassed by the consequences of the Kansas-Nebraska Act. When he left office, President Pierce was very unpopular in the North because of the issue of slavery. Sadly, his unpopularity and personal struggles with depression caused Mr. Pierce to start drinking a lot of alcohol again. Unfortunately, this resulted in him dying from a sickness called edema in 1869. He was sixty-four years old.

Although many problems arose while he was president, Franklin Pierce did succeed in making America bigger by purchasing new **territories**.

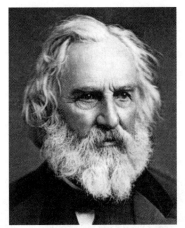
Henry Wadsworth Longfellow

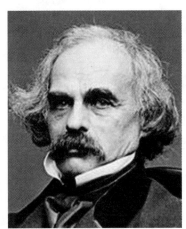
Nathaniel Hawthorne

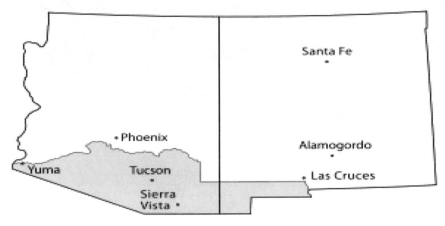
Gadsden Purchase - southern parts of Arizona and New Mexico

REVIEW BITES

VOCABULARY

College – A school that people attend when they are older to learn how to do certain jobs

Coward – Someone who gets easily scared of things

Purchase – Something that a person buys

Territories – Pieces of land that are not states

FUN FACT

An inaugural address is the first speech that someone gives after becoming president. Franklin Pierce's inaugural address was 3,319 words long, and he memorized the entire thing.

REVIEW QUESTIONS

1. Franklin Pierce fought during what war?

2. While he was president, what law did Franklin Pierce sign that caused fighting in Kansas and Nebraska?

3. What caused Franklin Pierce to get very sick and die?

James Buchanan
(1857–1861)

James Buchanan

James Buchanan was born in Pennsylvania in 1791. His parents were Irish immigrants. Sadly, when James was still young, his father died, leaving James' mother to care for eleven children. James had four brothers and six sisters.

When he was sixteen years old, James went to Dickenson College to learn how to be an **attorney**, and he graduated after two years. After college, James worked as a trial lawyer and eventually got into politics.

Mr. Buchanan started his career in politics when he was elected as a state representative in Pennsylvania. He went on to hold many other government positions. He served in the U.S. House of Representatives for a few years, and then President Andrew Jackson appointed him to be a **minister** to Russia.

Later, in 1834, Mr. Buchanan was elected into the U.S. Senate and worked there for eleven years. While James Polk was America's president, Mr. Buchanan served as his secretary of state. While in that position, he made important agreements with other countries and also made important decisions for America. In one situation, he tried to resolve disputes with Mexico about the southern border of Texas. These disputes eventually led to the Mexican-American War.

In 1848, Mr. Buchanan left politics for a few years and went home to take care of his twenty-two nieces and nephews. A few years later, in 1853, President Pierce appointed Mr. Buchanan as the minister to England.

In 1856, Mr. Buchanan ran for president as a Democrat and won easily. One of the main reasons he won was because he told people that he would help keep America united. Sadly, however, the country divided while he was president.

One thing that led to the country separating was a Supreme Court **case** called the Dred Scott Decision. A slave named Dred Scott said that he wanted to be an American citizen. However, the Supreme Court judges decided that Dred Scott could not be a legal citizen because he was a slave. President Buchanan stood by the decision because he wanted to follow the law, even though he disliked slavery. This made many Americans in the North very angry with President Buchanan.

In 1860, several Southern states decided to separate from America (secede from the Union). However, President Buchanan did nothing to stop this from happening, which made many Northerners angry with him.

In spite of these troubles, President Buchanan was able to make some important agreements with other countries. One example is that he prevented Great Britain from forming colonies in Central America, in accordance with the Monroe Doctrine (see section 5). He also opened sea ports on the west coast of America, which opened up trade with Asia.

Interestingly, Mr. Buchanan was the only president who never got married. He was going to marry a woman named Ann Coleman, but she died before he could. He vowed never to marry after that.

After his presidency, Mr. Buchanan went back home to Pennsylvania. He died in 1868 at the age of seventy-seven.

Dred Scott

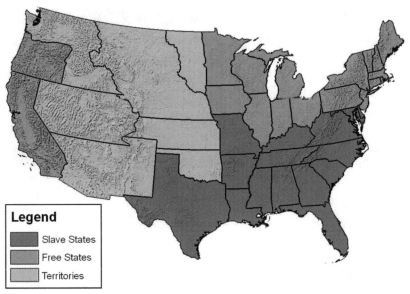

Division of the Northern and Southern states

REVIEW BITES

VOCABULARY

Attorney – Another word for lawyer; a person who practices law

Minister – A head of a government department who represents their country in other countries

Case – A legal action or law suit regarding a particular situation

Citizen – A person who is a member of a country

FUN FACT

One time, the Prince of Wales came to stay at the White House. He brought so many people with him that President Buchanan had to give up his own bedroom and sleep in the hallway.

89

REVIEW QUESTIONS

1. James Buchanan served as a minister to which two countries?

2. What made the North so angry with President Buchanan?

3. During his presidency, with what continent did James Buchanan open trade agreements?

1. Russia and England
2. He supported the Dred Scott Decision 3. Asia

Abraham Lincoln

Mary Lincoln

Abraham Lincoln was born in Hodgenville, Kentucky on February 12, 1809. Abraham's parents were very poor and lived in a log cabin in the woods. His mother died when Abraham was still young.

Although he only had one year of schooling at home, Abraham was able to read a few different books, including the Bible and books on American history.

In 1830, Abraham was in charge of a **ferryboat** and he delivered supplies up and down the Ohio River. Two years later, in 1832, he became a captain in the Black Hawk War.

After the war, Mr. Lincoln decided to become a **lawyer** and was known for being fair and honest to people. That is why he is known as "Honest Abe." During this time, he was also elected into the U.S. House of Representatives in Washington, D.C. Mr. Lincoln also ran for a seat in the U.S. Senate against a man named Stephen Douglas. They had many **debates** with each other, which became famous and are known as "The Lincoln-Douglas Debates." Although he lost the race for U.S. Senate, Mr. Lincoln became well known with the American people because of his speeches.

In 1842, Mr. Lincoln married Mary Todd, and they had four sons. Sadly, three of their boys died before the age of eighteen. This caused Mrs. Lincoln to be very sad for the rest of her life.

In 1854, a new political party was formed called the Republican Party. At their **convention** in 1860, the Republicans made Mr. Lincoln their first candidate to run for president. He beat three other men, winning the election in 1860. Because of this victory, he became the first official Republican president.

Due to some events during James Buchanan's presidency, the country was divided when Mr. Lincoln became president. In 1861, Southern soldiers attacked Fort Sumter in South Carolina, and this marked the official beginning of the Civil War, also known as the War Between the States.

During this war, in September of 1862, President Lincoln issued the Emancipation Proclamation, which freed the slaves in the southern/Confederate states. However, since the South had seceded from the Union and now had their own president (Jefferson Davis), they did not have to obey the laws of the North and no slaves were actually set free.

In 1863, President Lincoln gave a famous speech in Gettysburg, Pennsylvania where a big battle of the Civil War had taken place. His speech was called the "Gettysburg Address." It is one of the shortest, yet most famous speeches in American history.

For a while it seemed like the South would win the war, but then President Lincoln assigned a new general to the North, Ulysses S. Grant. Under General Grant's leadership, the North started to win and eventually defeated the South in April of 1865. By this time, President Lincoln had been elected to a second term. Now that the war was over, President Lincoln wanted to bring America back together again.

Sadly, on April 14, 1865, a man named John Wilkes Booth shot President Lincoln. Mr. Booth had been very angry about the South losing the war, and he hated

President Lincoln because of it. Mr. Lincoln died the next day, which made him the first president to be assassinated while in office.

Some people think that Abraham Lincoln is the best president because he helped the North win the Civil War, which gave slaves the right to freedom. However, in order to accomplish that, President Lincoln did some things that were unconstitutional, which means that he was not given the power to do them according to the Constitution. This caused great controversy in America. Interestingly, the thirteenth amendment, which officially abolished slavery, was not actually passed until several months after President Lincoln died.

Penny

President Lincoln
with Northern/Union soldiers

Five dollar bill

The Lincoln Memorial in Washington, D.C.

REVIEW BITES

VOCABULARY

Ferryboat – A boat used to carry people or supplies

Lawyer – Another word for attorney; a person who practices law

Debates – Discussions and/or arguments between people with differing opinions

Convention – A place where many people meet to discuss and decide important things

FUN FACT

Abraham Lincoln loved his sons very much. Many times, they would come into the Oval Office and wrestle on the floor with their father.

REVIEW QUESTIONS

1. While running for a seat in the U.S. Senate, with whom did Abraham Lincoln have famous debates?

2. Abraham Lincoln was the first person to be elected as a member of what political party?

3. What document did President Lincoln create that was supposed to help free the slaves in the South?

17

Andrew Johnson
(1865-1869)

Andrew Johnson

Eliza Johnson

Andrew Johnson was born in North Carolina in 1808. Sadly, Andrew's father died while trying to save two drowning men in an icy river, leaving Andrew's mother to take care of the family alone. After Mr. Johnson's death, the family became very poor, and the townspeople made fun of them for it.

To help provide money for his family, Andrew learned how to be a **tailor**. He worked for seven years and then moved to Tennessee. While he was there, Andrew opened up his own tailor shop. People came to Andrew's shop to discuss the latest news along with what was happening in the government. This made Andrew and his shop popular in that area.

In 1827, Mr. Johnson married Eliza McCardle, and they had five children together. Since Andrew had never attended school, Eliza taught him many different subjects, including reading and math.

When he was twenty years old, Mr. Johnson was elected as a member of his city's court. After that, he became the mayor of Greenville, Tennessee. He was then elected as part of Tennessee's state legislature. Later, in 1841 and 1857, Mr. Johnson was elected into the U.S. Senate and the House of Representatives. He also served as the governor of Tennessee in between his times in Congress.

As a result of holding many different government positions, Andrew Johnson became well known. In 1865, Abraham Lincoln chose Mr. Johnson to be his vice presidential candidate. Even though Abraham Lincoln was a Republican and Andrew Johnson was a Democrat, the Republicans wanted Mr. Johnson because he could help persuade Democrats to vote for Abraham Lincoln. Because of this, Abraham Lincoln won the election, and Mr. Johnson became America's vice president.

When President Lincoln was shot and killed in April of 1865, Vice President Andrew Johnson became the next president. Mr. Johnson had a big job to do. After the Civil War, he had to help bring the country back together again. This time period is known as **Reconstruction.** The United States Congress developed many plans for helping the country unite again, but President Johnson vetoed many of the plans because he did not agree with them. However, Congress was able to get some of the plans passed, and by the time President Johnson left office, most of the Southern states had rejoined America again.

During this time, Congress made a law called the Tenure of Office Act. This made it illegal for President Johnson to remove any of his officeholders or cabinet members without Congress' approval. President Johnson disobeyed this law, and because of that, Congress tried to get him impeached (removed from office). However, President Johnson remained in office because his impeachment failed to win the two-thirds majority in the Senate by only one vote. This was the first time an attempt was made to impeach an American president.

One notable achievement was that President Johnson and a man named William Seward bought land from Russia. This land became the state of Alaska and, as a result, made America much bigger.

In 1869, Andrew Johnson's presidency ended. In 1874, he was elected again into the U.S. Senate. Soon afterwards, Mr. Johnson died in 1875 at the age of sixty-six.

William Seward

Andrew Johnson's impeachment trial

Alaska

REVIEW BITES

VOCABULARY

Tailor – Someone who makes and mends people's clothes

Mayor – The leader of a city's government

Governor – Someone who leads a state or territory

Reconstruction – The process of bringing the Southern states back into America

FUN FACT

Even after becoming a state legislator, Andrew Johnson continued making his own clothes.

REVIEW QUESTIONS

1. What was Andrew Johnson's first job?

2. Andrew Johnson was the governor of which state?

3. What large piece of land was purchased from Russia during Andrew Johnson's presidency?

1. Tailor 2. Tennessee 3. Alaska

18

Ulysses S. Grant (1869-1877)

Ulysses S. Grant

Julia Grant

Hiram Ulysses Grant was born in Ohio on April 27, 1822. He grew up in a small log cabin with five siblings.

When he was seventeen years old, he attended a military academy called West Point. While enrolling, his name was accidentally written as Ulysses Simpson Grant. People called him that for the rest of his life. While at West Point, Ulysses learned how to be a soldier. He graduated in 1843.

In 1846, Mr. Grant joined the U.S. Army and fought during the Mexican-American War. He started out as a second lieutenant and was brevetted (appointed) captain by the end of the war.

In 1848, after the Mexican-American War ended, Mr. Grant married a woman named Julia Dent. Interestingly, Ulysses' family did not like slavery, but Julia's family owned slaves. Because of this, neither of their families approved of their marriage. They had four children together.

When the Civil War began in 1861, Mr. Grant became a leader of Northern soldiers and won many battles, including one at Fort Donelson, Tennessee. Because of Mr. Grant's leadership, President Abraham Lincoln made him the leader of the entire Northern Army. After that, General Grant won many more battles and eventually defeated the South in 1865. After this, Southern General Robert E. Lee surrendered to General Grant.

In 1868, because of his popularity after the Civil War, Mr. Grant was elected as America's eighteenth president. In 1872, President Grant was elected to a second term.

While he was president, Mr. Grant had many problems. In 1873, because of a national financial crisis, many American businesses and banks had to close, which made many people lose all of their money. This was called the Panic of 1873. However, President Grant used America's gold to help pay back a lot of the debt.

Unfortunately, many **scandals** occurred during Mr. Grant's presidency. Many of his helpers were liars and cheaters, who stole money from America's government. However, President Grant did not know what they were doing most of the time.

When his terms ended in 1877, President Grant had become very unpopular in some parts of the country. This was because of the Panic of 1873 and the scandals of his administration. One of the positive things he accomplished was signing the Civil Rights Act of 1875, which prohibited the unfair treatment of black people with regards to housing and transportation. However, in 1883, the Supreme Court declared the act unconstitutional because they said that Congress did not have the authority to regulate people's private affairs.

After his presidency ended, Ulysses S. Grant wrote a book about his life, called <u>The Autobiography of General Ulysses S. Grant</u>. He died on July 23, 1885, at age sixty-three, just a few days after completing the book.

General Robert E. Lee surrendering to General Ulysses S. Grant

Fifty dollar bill

Cannons at Fort Donelson in Tennessee

REVIEW BITES

VOCABULARY

Graduated – When one has completed school and received a diploma (a piece of paper that you get once you finish at a school)

Lieutenant – A type of leader in the military, who commands a certain number of soldiers

Surrendered – Gave up

Scandal – An affair that usually brings disgrace (embarrassment) to someone

FUN FACT

One time, a policeman gave President Grant a speeding ticket for driving his horse-drawn carriage too fast. President Grant had to walk back to the White House.

REVIEW QUESTIONS

1. At what military school did Ulysses S. Grant learn how to be a soldier?

2. During the Civil War, which army did Ulysses S. Grant lead?

3. What caused many scandals during Ulysses S. Grant's presidency?

19

Rutherford B. Hayes (1877–1881)

Rutherford B. Hayes

Lucy Hayes

Rutherford Birchard Hayes was born in Delaware, Ohio in 1822. When he was young, his uncle paid for him to go to school. Rutherford was a weak child, but he grew up to be very strong and healthy.

After he finished school, Rutherford attended Kenyon College where he became the top student in his class. In 1842, Rutherford attended a very famous **law school** called Harvard University. Shortly after graduating in 1845, he began to work as a volunteer **attorney** for the Underground Railroad. This was a secret way to help slaves escape the South and get to the North. Rutherford's job was to help defend the slaves and workers on the Underground Railroad.

Mr. Hayes also helped to establish the Republican branch in the Ohio government. During this time, he became friends with some powerful Ohio **politicians** who helped Mr. Hayes with some of his future elections.

Several years earlier, Mr. Hayes had met a young woman named Lucy Webb, who was only fourteen years old. She went on to finish school and graduate from college. They eventually got married in December of 1852, and they had eight children together.

In 1861, when the Civil War began, Mr. Hayes became a soldier in the Northern army. By the end of the war, he had become an important leader because of his bravery and strategic planning.

In 1868, three years after the Civil War ended, Mr. Hayes became Ohio's governor. He was elected as governor three times and then decided to run for president in 1876.

The election of 1876 was very unique. Mr. Hayes was a Republican and won by only one **electoral vote**. His opponent was a Democrat named Samuel Tilden. Each of them had received about half of the popular votes, but there was much controversy surrounding the election. There was proof of fraud on both sides. To resolve the issue, Congress decided to make Mr. Hayes the next president, and this is known as the Compromise of 1877. Part of the compromise was that the Democrats would let the Republicans win, so long as there were Democrats helping Mr. Hayes while he was president.

Because Presidents Johnson and Grant had many problems while they were president, they had become unpopular with many Americans. President Hayes worked to bring honesty back to the office of the president. He did this by giving government jobs to trustworthy people who deserved them.

Also, while Ulysses S. Grant had been president, the Panic of 1873 occurred in which many people lost all of their money. President Hayes helped improve the economy by backing the dollar with the federal gold reserve.

In 1881, after his presidency ended, Mr. Hayes went back to his home in Ohio, called Spiegel Grove. While there, he helped to establish Ohio State University, Ohio Wesleyan College, and the Western Reserve University.

Rutherford B. Hayes died at his home in 1893 at the age of seventy.

Smithsonian exhibit of
President Hayes on a telephone

Ohio State University

REVIEW BITES

VOCABULARY

Law school – Where someone learns how to be a lawyer

Attorney – Another word for lawyer; a person who practices law

Politicians – People who lead a government

Electoral Vote – A vote from the electoral college (a voting system for each state and the entire country)

Economy – The amount of goods and services a country produces and consumes

FUN FACT

While Rutherford B. Hayes was president, the first telephone was installed in the White House. Interestingly, President Hayes' phone number was simply the number "1."

☆☆☆☆☆☆☆☆☆☆

REVIEW QUESTIONS

1. Rutherford B. Hayes worked as an attorney for what secret system for slaves?

2. Rutherford B. Hayes was an important leader during what war?

3. By how many electoral votes did Rutherford B. Hayes win the presidential election?

1. The Underground Railroad
2. The Civil War 3. One

James A. Garfield

Lucretia Garfield

James A. Garfield was born in Orange, Ohio on November 19, 1831. His father, Abram, died when James was still a baby. His mother later married another man, but James never grew close to him.

James learned how to read when he was only three years old and did very well in school. Even though his family was poor, James went to Ohio Western Reserve Eclectic Institute (now Hiram College) and became the leader of a **literary** group there. In 1858, James finished his time at another school called William's College. While there, he did especially well in Latin, reading, and sports.

After college, Mr. Garfield became a **preacher** and traveled around Ohio speaking against slavery. Because of this, he is known as "The Preacher President." As a result of his preaching, Mr. Garfield became well known for his **public speaking** skills. Eventually, he went back to his old school, Ohio Western Reserve Eclectic Institute and became its president.

One of Mr. Garfield's childhood friends was Lucretia Rudolph. They got married in 1858 and had seven children together. Sadly, their daughter, Eliza, died when she was only three years old.

In 1861, when the Civil War began, Mr. Garfield became a **colonel** in the Northern army and led many men into battle. Two years later, he was elected into the U.S. House of Representatives and became the minority leader. This meant that he was in charge of the Republican Party, and they were the smaller of the two political parties at the time (which is why he was called the "minority" leader).

In 1880, the Republicans nominated Mr. Garfield as their candidate for president. He gave speeches near and at his home, and he won the election by a small margin. He defeated a Democrat named Winfield Scott Hancock, who had been a popular general during the Civil War.

A man named Charles Guiteau had given speeches to help James Garfield get elected as president. Because of this, Mr. Guiteau thought that he should be able to have a job in the government. However, President Garfield would not give him a job because he was refusing to grant any requests from his friends for government positions. This made Charles Guiteau very angry.

People later learned that Mr. Guiteau had become insane (crazy) with anger. As a result, he took revenge on President Garfield and assassinated him just months after he was elected president. Sadly, President Garfield died a few weeks later in September of 1881.

We do not know what James Garfield would have accomplished as president. However, he did believe in ending the practice of patronage appointments (which is when a president gives his friends government jobs). He also believed that the president should be allowed to make decisions on his own without the approval of Congress.

James A. Garfield in his
Civil War uniform

General Winfield Scott Hancock

James A. Garfield's inauguration

REVIEW BITES

VOCABULARY

Literary – Having to do with reading or literature

Preacher – A man who tells people the truth about the Bible and Jesus Christ during a sermon in church

Public speaking – Speaking in front of a group of people

Colonel – A type of leader in the military, who commands a certain number of soldiers

FUN FACT

James Garfield was very talented and could write with both hands. He could write a word in Latin with one hand while simultaneously writing it in Greek with the other.

REVIEW QUESTIONS

1. Why was James Garfield called "The Preacher President?"

2. James Garfield served as a colonel during what war?

3. Why was President Garfield assassinated?

1. Because he had been a preacher in Ohio 2. The Civil War
3. Because he did not give a job to a man named Charles Guiteau

Chester A. Arthur
(1881-1885)

Chester A. Arthur

Ellen Arthur

Chester Alan Arthur was born in Fairfield, Vermont in 1829 but grew up in upstate New York. As a child, he was very **rebellious**. While at school, he would often fight with other children. One time, Chester even convinced some children to dump the school bell into the Erie Canal.

After he finished school, Chester went to Union College. When he finished college, Chester moved to New York City to become a lawyer. While there, he helped to defend black people's rights and freedoms. At that time, black people were not allowed to use the same means of public transportation as white people. Mr. Arthur fought hard to change this.

Around that same time, Mr. Arthur met a woman named Ellen Herndon. They got married in 1859 and eventually had three children together. Sadly, Mrs. Arthur died before her husband became president, and Mr. Arthur never remarried.

During the Civil War, Mr. Arthur led the New York militia, which was a small army of men from the state of New York. His job was to give soldiers clothing, armament, and other supplies they needed for the war.

In 1871, Mr. Arthur was appointed collector for the New York **Customs** House. His job was to make sure that other countries that were trading with America paid the proper taxes on their goods. Mr. Arthur worked at this job for seven years. However, in 1878, he was **fired** because he did not follow a new law that President Rutherford B. Hayes had made regarding the patronage system. This system allowed politicians to hire their friends and relatives even if they had no experience for that job. President Hayes reformed the system and said that these things were no longer allowed. Mr. Arthur ignored this new law, kept hiring his friends, and consequently got fired for it.

In 1880, the Republicans chose Mr. Arthur as James Garfield's vice presidential candidate. They did this because some people liked Mr. Arthur and would therefore vote for James Garfield. Mr. Garfield was elected as president in 1880 but sadly was shot a few months later and died. Mr. Arthur then became the next president.

As president, Mr. Arthur eliminated the patronage system, which shocked many people because he had previously supported it. Instead, President Arthur made people take tests first to see if they were actually qualified for a government job. Initially, Americans did not trust President Arthur, but that slowly changed as he worked to end government corruption. President Arthur also helped to decrease America's **national debt**.

One other important thing to note is that before Mr. Arthur was president, America's fighting ships were all made out of wood. President Arthur recognized the danger in this and had a new fleet of ships built out of steel. These ships were much stronger than the old ones and helped to strengthen America's Navy.

Chester Arthur died in November of 1886, only one year after his presidency ended. He was fifty-seven years old.

Original steel U.S. Navy ship

Modern day U.S. Navy ship

REVIEW BITES

VOCABULARY

Rebellious – Going against authority and not obeying rules

Customs – A tax on goods from another country

Fired – Forced to give up a job

National debt – The amount of money that a country has borrowed

FUN FACT

President Arthur owned over eighty pairs of pants and changed his clothes many times a day. Because of this, he was called "Elegant Arthur."

REVIEW QUESTIONS

1. In what city was Chester Arthur a lawyer?

2. During the Civil War, which state's militia did Chester Arthur lead?

3. What system did President Arthur eliminate?

1. New York City 2. New York's 3. The Patronage System

Grover Cleveland

Frances Cleveland

Stephen Grover Cleveland was born in New Jersey in 1837. As a boy, he preferred to be called Grover instead of Stephen.

Grover started school at eleven years old and later attended Hamilton College. Sadly, while he was in college, his father died. Because of this, Grover's mother could not afford his college tuition. So, Grover went to New York and became a teacher. He decided to move out west, but while on his way, he stopped in the city of Buffalo, New York and ended up staying there permanently.

While he was in Buffalo, Mr. Cleveland became a lawyer and a sheriff. People liked him because he worked hard to eliminate **crime**.

Unlike some of the previous presidents, Mr. Cleveland never fought in the Civil War. When the war began, Mr. Cleveland paid someone else (a Polish immigrant) to go and fight for him. This was completely legal for him to do under the Federal Conscription Act.

In 1881, the people in Buffalo elected Mr. Cleveland as their mayor. He became very popular and was later elected as the governor of New York in 1882.

Since he was so popular in New York, the Democrats chose him as their candidate for the next presidential election. However, when he ran for president in 1884, Mr. Cleveland faced many problems. He was a Democrat, and the Republicans discovered that he had done something controversial earlier in his life. They tried to use this against him, but because Mr. Cleveland was so popular, he won the presidential election anyway.

During his first term, President Cleveland worked to help Native Americans buy land in America and also helped to make America's **debt** smaller. He did this by stopping the people in Congress from spending too much money. As a result, America's debt decreased during his presidency.

In 1886, while he was president, Mr. Cleveland married Frances Folsom in the White House. They had five children together.

In 1888, President Cleveland ran for a second consecutive **term** against Benjamin Harrison but lost. Four years later, in 1892, Mr. Cleveland ran against Benjamin Harrison again and won. Mr. Cleveland and his wife, Frances, went back to the White House in 1893. Grover Cleveland was the only president to serve two non-consecutive terms. This means that his two terms were not in a row or back to back.

During his second term, the Panic of 1893 occurred. This caused many businesses and banks to lose all of their money. President Cleveland refused to have the federal government help because he thought the country could fix itself. This made Mr. Cleveland very unpopular with many people and caused him to not be reelected as president.

In 1897, Grover Cleveland went back to New Jersey and died there on June 24, 1908, at age seventy-one.

Grover Cleveland marrying Frances Folsom in the White House

One thousand dollar bill

Baby Ruth candy bar
(see "Fun Fact" on next page)

REVIEW BITES

VOCABULARY

Crime – Things that people do which break the law

Debt – Money that people or a country owe to someone else

Term – The time that someone serves as an elected official

FUN FACT

One of Grover Cleveland's five children was named Ruth. The candy bar "Baby Ruth" was named after her.

REVIEW QUESTIONS

1. In what city was Grover Cleveland a sheriff and a mayor?

2. What was different about Grover Cleveland's terms compared to other presidents?

3. During Grover Cleveland's second term in 1893, many businesses and banks lost all of their money. What was this called?

Benjamin Harrison

Caroline Harrison

Benjamin Harrison was born in Ohio on August 20, 1833. Benjamin Harrison was called "Little Ben" because he was only five feet six inches tall. Benjamin's grandfather was William Henry Harrison, America's ninth president.

While in school, Benjamin did very well in **debates** with other people. This helped him become a good **public speaker** later in life. After he finished school, Benjamin thought about becoming a preacher. However, he decided to go to college to become a lawyer instead. In 1852, he graduated from Miami University in Ohio.

In 1853, Mr. Harrison married Caroline Scott, and they had three children together. Sadly, Caroline died shortly before her husband's presidency ended in 1892. Eventually, Mr. Harrison got married again to a woman named Mary Dimmick, his late wife's niece.

During the Civil War, Mr. Harrison joined the Northern army. He became a **brigadier general** for his bravery and many victories during the war. He led his soldiers into many different battles, including the Battle of Nashville.

After the war, Mr. Harrison tried to become the governor of Indiana twice but lost both times. However, in 1881, he was elected into the U.S. Senate.

In 1888, the Republicans chose Mr. Harrison as their candidate for U.S. president. Mr. Harrison defeated President Grover Cleveland by a small margin.

President Harrison was called "The Billion Dollar President" because in one year during his presidency, he created a one billion dollar spending budget. Some of the money went to the soldiers who fought for the North during the Civil War. Another part of the money went to making America's Navy bigger and stronger.

President Harrison also signed the McKinley Tariff of 1890, which made countries pay more money in taxes for supplies they were trading with America. Another law that President Harrison signed was the Land Revision Act of 1891. This allowed the president to set aside land for national parks. As a result, President Harrison was able to set aside land for Yellowstone Park in Wyoming later in his presidency.

Also, while Mr. Harrison was president, six more states were added to America: North Dakota, South Dakota, Wyoming, Montana, Washington, and Idaho.

In 1892, Mr. Harrison ran for president again but this time lost to Grover Cleveland. So, he went back home to Indiana and wrote two books: <u>This Country of Ours</u> and <u>Views of an Ex-President</u>. During this time, Mr. Harrison gave many speeches across the country and also worked for Presidents Cleveland and McKinley.

Benjamin Harrison died of pneumonia on March 13, 1901, in Indianapolis, Indiana. He was sixty-seven years old.

Benjamin Harrison
during the Civil War

Benjamin Harrison's inauguration

Yellowstone National Park; 63 miles x 54 miles big; 2,219,789 acres

REVIEW BITES

VOCABULARY

Debates – Discussions and/or arguments between people with differing opinions

Public Speaker – Someone who speaks in front of a group of people

Brigadier General – A type of leader in the military, who commands a certain number of soldiers

FUN FACT

During Benjamin Harrison's presidency, lightbulbs were installed in the White House for the first time. One time, President Harrison got shocked by one, and after that, he and his wife were afraid of the lights.

REVIEW QUESTIONS

1. Before becoming a lawyer, what did Benjamin Harrison want to be?

2. Benjamin Harrison tried twice to become the governor of which state?

3. How much money did President Harrison spend for one year's budget?

1. Preacher 2. Indiana 3. One billion dollars

138

William McKinley

Ida McKinley

William McKinley was born in Ohio on January 29, 1843. He grew up with eight brothers and sisters and went to Poland Academy. When he started school, William was very shy and did not like talking to people. However, he did very well in school and eventually was not shy anymore. In fact, William became a great public speaker. Ever since he was young, William always thought that one day he would become the president of the United States.

After high school, William enrolled at Allegheny College but had to withdraw soon afterwards due to exhaustion, illness, and a lack of money. He then decided to work as a postal clerk and part-time teacher instead.

In 1861, when the Civil War began, William joined the Northern army. Interestingly, during some battles, he was led by Brevet Major General Rutherford B. Hayes, who eventually became America's nineteenth president.

Once the Civil War ended, Mr. McKinley tried to become a lawyer but failed. So, he decided to go into politics instead. In 1867, he became a county chairman for the Republicans. He was also elected into the U.S. Congress and eventually became the governor of Ohio.

In 1871, Mr. McKinley married a woman named Ida Saxton, and they had two children together.

In 1896, Mr. McKinley ran for president as a Republican. During his campaign, he switched his views on the monetary system, which led many businesses to support him. He also printed two hundred million pamphlets in fourteen different languages and distributed them all across America. Both of these things helped him to get elected.

In 1898, while William McKinley was president, the Spanish-American War began. Spain had control over an island called Cuba, and Cuba wanted to become its own country. So, President McKinley sent a ship, called the USS Maine, to help the Cubans. Shockingly, the ship exploded after it arrived in Cuba, and many people thought that the Spanish had done it. Because of this, President McKinley **declared war** on Spain and sent soldiers to fight the Spanish in Cuba. The Americans defeated the Spanish in just a few months. As a result, Spain agreed to put Puerto Rico, Guam, and the Philippines under America's control in exchange for twenty million dollars. By winning this war, America showed the world that it was a powerful country.

In addition to America's success in the Spanish-American War, the U.S. economy started to recover after the Panic of 1893. This happened as a result of President McKinley relaxing government interference in business.

In 1900, Mr. McKinley was elected to a second term as president. He then went to Buffalo, New York, to begin a **speaking tour**. Sadly, while he was there, a man named Leon Czolgosz shot him. Mr. Czolgosz was an anarchist and was part of a movement that wanted to kill important leaders just for the sake of creating chaos.

President McKinley died eight days later on September 14, 1901, at age fifty-eight. His vice president,

Theodore Roosevelt, was on a family vacation in the Adirondack Mountains when he heard the news that President McKinley had died. He rushed to Buffalo and was inaugurated in a close friend's home there, which is now a historical museum.

USS Maine

USS Maine *Memorial*

Five hundred dollar bill

Theodore Roosevelt's inaugural site in Buffalo, New York

REVIEW BITES

VOCABULARY

Declared war – Announced that there would be a war with another country

Speaking tour – A trip on which someone gives speeches

FUN FACT

President McKinley had a pet parrot which could whistle the tune of "Yankee Doodle." The president would start whistling the first half of the song, and his parrot would finish the rest.

REVIEW QUESTIONS

1. During the Civil War, who led William McKinley in some battles?

2. What war occurred while William McKinley was president?

3. In what city was William McKinley assassinated?

Theodore Roosevelt

Edith Roosevelt

Theodore Roosevelt was born in New York City in October of 1858. While growing up, Theodore had many health problems. He was sick most of the time and suffered from stomach aches, painful headaches, and asthma. Theodore tried many things to get better, but most of them did not help. His father told him to exercise more, so Theodore obeyed his father and began to get better. He especially enjoyed swimming, hiking, and boxing and really loved being outdoors.

In addition to sports, Theodore also loved reading

about American history. After finishing school, he attended Harvard University.

In 1880, Theodore graduated from college and thought about becoming a lawyer but decided to go into politics instead. Around this same time, he married a woman named Alice Hathaway Lee.

In 1882, Mr. Roosevelt was elected as a New York State assemblyman. While in New York, he also worked as a policeman and was eventually elected as the police commissioner of New York City.

In 1884, Theodore and his wife, Alice, had their first child together. Sadly, two days after the birth of their daughter, Alice died. Tragically, earlier that same day, Theodore's mother had also died. Theodore was so distraught over the deaths of his mother and wife that he left his life in New York and headed west to become a cattle rancher for two years in the Dakota territory. He left his infant daughter in the care of his sister, Anna.

Two years later, in 1886, Theodore married a woman named Edith Carow. His young daughter then moved back home with him and Edith. Theodore and Edith went on to have five of their own children together.

In 1897, Mr. Roosevelt went to work as assistant secretary of the U.S. Navy under President William McKinley. When the Spanish-American War began in

1898, Mr. Roosevelt gathered a fighting group together called "The Rough Riders." They fought in Cuba and won an important battle on San Juan Hill. This made Mr. Roosevelt very famous and helped him to become William McKinley's vice presidential candidate during President McKinley's second term.

After President McKinley was shot and killed in 1901, Mr. Roosevelt immediately became America's next president. During his presidency, he tried to stop big businesses from taking over smaller businesses. He was also opposed to the government controlling businesses and wanted **capitalism** to be free to grow.

President Roosevelt made many foreign policy agreements. One agreement included overseeing the construction of the Panama Canal, which is a waterway that connects the Atlantic Ocean and the Pacific Ocean across Latin America. This was important because it allowed boats to travel more quickly to different places of the world, helping to increase trade between countries.

President Roosevelt also helped to create many of America's National Parks under the Forest Reserve Act, including Yosemite National Park. Because of this, forests, mountains, and animals were protected and preserved for recreational use.

After his two terms ended in 1909, President

Roosevelt took a trip to Europe. After he returned to America, he ran for president again in 1912 against Woodrow Wilson and William Howard Taft but lost.

Theodore Roosevelt continued to explore and travel to many different places. He died on January 6, 1919, in New York at the age of sixty.

Boy with teddy bear, which was named after President Theodore, "Teddy," Roosevelt

Theodore Roosevelt and the Rough Riders

Half Dome Rock in Yosemite National Park in California

REVIEW BITES

VOCABULARY

Commissioner – A person in charge of a department or district

Capitalism – An economic system that features private ownership of businesses and encourages personal income and profit

FUN FACT

President Roosevelt created many expressions, including "Good to the last drop!" This became the Maxwell House Coffee slogan. (President Roosevelt drank up to a gallon of coffee every day.)

REVIEW QUESTIONS

1. In what war did Theodore Roosevelt lead his "Rough Riders"?

2. What waterway's construction began during Theodore Roosevelt's presidency?

3. What was created under the Forest Reserve Act?

1. The Spanish-American War 2. The Panama Canal
3. National Parks

William Howard Taft

Helen Taft

William Howard Taft was born in Cincinnati, Ohio in 1857. Ever since he was young, William was very overweight and this led to him having many health problems. Sadly, people also made fun of his weight.

As a teenager, William believed that women should have the right to vote in elections. This was a very unpopular idea in some parts of America at that time.

After he finished school, William attended Yale University. William did well in college and finished second in his class. In 1878, he graduated from Yale and went on to study law at Cincinnati Law School. From then on, William always wanted to serve as a judge on America's highest court, the Supreme Court.

In 1886, Mr. Taft married a woman named Helen ("Nellie") Herron, and they had three children together.

In 1900, President William McKinley asked Mr. Taft to be part of a group called the "Philippine Commission." The Philippines are a group of islands near Asia that America purchased after the Spanish-American War. Mr. Taft was appointed as governor of the Philippines.

In 1904, Mr. Taft returned to America and worked as President Theodore Roosevelt's secretary of war. Mr. Taft helped to make decisions about America's involvement with other countries.

In 1908, Mr. Taft decided to run for president. Even though he was not really interested in doing this, his wife, Helen, and President Theodore Roosevelt strongly encouraged him to run. Mrs. Taft worked very hard to help her husband get elected. Also, since President Roosevelt was so popular with the American people, and he endorsed Mr. Taft, Mr. Taft won the election by a large margin.

During his presidency, Mr. Taft continued some of the same policies that Theodore Roosevelt had begun, such as stopping big businesses from taking over smaller ones. This was known as "trust-busting." However, unlike Theodore Roosevelt, President Taft did not want to show the world America's power and strength and believed in being peaceful toward other countries. So, he began a program called "Dollar Diplomacy." In this program, President Taft gave money to support other countries and began trading agreements with some of them.

President Taft also created many new government groups, including the Department of Labor and the Bureau of Mines. President Taft also helped to create the federal income tax.

In 1912, Mr. Taft ran for a second term as president but lost. Eventually, in 1921, his lifelong dream came true, and he was made the Chief Justice of the United States Supreme Court under President Warren Harding.

In 1930, one month after he retired from the Supreme Court, William Howard Taft died in Washington, D.C. from high blood pressure and heart disease. He was seventy-two years old.

William Howard Taft on a water buffalo in the Philippines

William Howard Taft on the Supreme Court

VOCABULARY

Income tax – Money that people have to pay to the government based on how much they earn at their job

FUN FACT

William Howard Taft loved baseball. In fact, he began the tradition of the president throwing out the first ball on baseball's opening day.

REVIEW QUESTIONS

1. Ever since he was young, William Taft dreamed of becoming a judge on what high court?

2. William Taft worked as the governor of what group of islands?

3. While president, what program did William Taft begin that involved trading with other countries?

1. The United States Supreme Court 2. The Philippines
3. "Dollar Diplomacy"

28

Woodrow Wilson
(1913-1921)

Woodrow Wilson

Edith Wilson

Thomas Woodrow Wilson was born in Virginia on December 29, 1856. Instead of "Thomas," he became known as "Woodrow" instead. Ever since he was young, Woodrow suffered from bad health, and because of this, he was homeschooled. Woodrow worked diligently at his schoolwork and eventually began college in 1873. He only stayed there for one year, though, because of his health problems.

Eventually, Woodrow was able to go back to college and decided to attend Princeton University in New Jersey. While there, he participated in sports and also in writing and speaking groups. In 1879, he graduated from Princeton and went on to John Hopkins University. In 1886, he graduated from John Hopkins University, earning a doctorate **degree**. This gave him the title "Dr." but did not make him a medical doctor. It is a title that a person earns when they complete a PhD degree in college. After earning his PhD, Mr. Wilson became the president of Princeton University.

In 1885, Woodrow married a woman named Ellen Axson and they had three children together. Ellen was Woodrow's wife for many years, but she died one year after he became president. In 1915, Mr. Wilson married another woman named Edith Galt.

Being the president at Princeton University helped Mr. Wilson gain popularity in New Jersey. In 1910, he became the governor of New Jersey.

In 1912, the Republican Party was divided. Some of the Republicans liked Theodore Roosevelt while others liked President William Taft. The Democratic Party saw this as an opportunity to win the next election, so they decided to nominate Woodrow Wilson as their presidential candidate. In 1912, Woodrow Wilson won the election in a **landslide** and became America's twenty-eighth president.

While he was president, Mr. Wilson began a new banking and business system, called the Federal Reserve System.

This meant the banking and business systems in America were now controlled by the federal government, which gave the government a lot of power.

In 1914, World War I began and involved many countries around the world, especially in Europe. Germany and Austria-Hungary were fighting against England, France, and Russia. President Wilson decided to not get America involved.

Many people liked how President Wilson kept America out of World War I. Because of this, he was reelected as president in 1916. However, only a few months later, President Wilson decided to enter the U.S. into the war after the Germans had sunk an American merchant ship.

During World War I, President Wilson signed laws that forced people to leave America if they were against the war. This is called **deportation**. He also sent government workers to spy on Americans who opposed the war because he wanted to make sure that people were loyal to America. However, by doing this, he took away some Americans' rights and freedoms to privacy and speech.

In 1918, World War I ended. After the war, President Wilson became sick, and his second wife, Edith, helped him with some of his presidential work.

In 1921, Woodrow Wilson's presidency ended. He died in 1924 in Washington, D.C. at age sixty-seven.

"Big Four" Leaders at the Paris Peace Conference, after the end of WWI;
from left to right: David Lloyd George (British Prime Minister),
Vittorio Emanuele Orlando (Italian Prime Minister), Georges Clemenceau
(French Prime Minister), and President Woodrow Wilson

100,000 dollar bill
(see "Fun Fact" on next page)

REVIEW BITES

VOCABULARY

Degree – A certificate that is given to someone when they have finished college

Landslide – When a person wins an election by a large number of votes

Deportation – When a government removes people from its country

FUN FACT

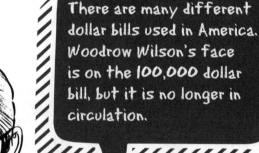

There are many different dollar bills used in America. Woodrow Wilson's face is on the 100,000 dollar bill, but it is no longer in circulation.

REVIEW QUESTIONS

1. Woodrow Wilson was the president of what college in New Jersey?

2. Woodrow Wilson was the governor of which state?

3. Woodrow Wilson was the president during what war?

29

Warren G. Harding
(1921–1923)

Warren G. Harding

Florence Harding

Warren Gamaliel Harding was born in Caledonia, Ohio on November 2, 1865. Caledonia was later renamed Blooming Grove, Ohio. As a young man, Warren got a job at a newspaper business. He later became a newspaper businessman himself.

Once he finished school, Warren attended Iberia College (now Ohio Central College) where he learned how to be a teacher. However, teaching was very challenging, and Warren decided to become a news reporter instead.

After a few years as a news reporter, Warren and

some of his friends decided to buy a newspaper business called *The Marion Star* in Marion, Ohio. This business worked out well, and it made Warren well known in the area. People liked that he reported the facts (truth) instead of his opinion. During this time, some newspaper writers would just write their opinions instead of reporting the facts.

Around this same time, Mr. Harding met his sister's piano teacher, Florence DeWolfe. They were eventually married in 1891 but never had any children together.

In 1899, Mr. Harding was elected to his first government position as an Ohio state senator. He helped to make decisions for the state of Ohio as a Republican.

In 1903, Mr. Harding was elected Ohio's lieutenant governor, and in 1914, he was elected to the U.S. Senate.

In 1920, the Republican Party chose Mr. Harding as their presidential candidate, and he accepted the nomination. He won the election by a large margin, mainly because he told people that he would help get things back to normal after World War I.

President Harding made a plan called "America First." This plan had five main elements (points) that included what he wanted to do with money, taxes, and immigration. Also, while Woodrow Wilson was president, he had many people put in jail for saying negative things against America's government, but President Harding later freed them.

While Mr. Harding was president, his Cabinet members (people who helped him make decisions) did many things that were against the law. Even though President Harding did not know about many of the secret deals his Cabinet members were making, he was still blamed for their choices.

During his presidency, Mr. Harding took a trip across the country. While on his way to Alaska, he became very sick and died in California on August 2, 1923. Although we are not sure how he died, doctors believed that President Harding suffered a heart attack. He was only fifty-seven years old. After this, his vice president, Calvin Coolidge, became president.

President Harding with famous baseball player, Babe Ruth

President Harding throwing the first ball at a baseball game

REVIEW BITES

VOCABULARY

Businessman — Someone who owns and runs a business

Opinion — What someone thinks or believes about something

Nomination — When someone is selected to run for a government office

FUN FACT

Compared to all of the other presidents, Warren Harding had the biggest feet and wore a size 14 shoe.

★ ★ ★ ★ ★ ★ ★ ★ ★ ★

REVIEW QUESTIONS

1. When he was young, what kind of business did Warren Harding own?

2. In which state was Warren Harding elected lieutenant governor?

3. What was President Harding's plan called regarding America's money, taxes, and immigration?

1. Newspaper 2. Ohio 3. "America First"

30

Calvin Coolidge (1923-1929)

Calvin Coolidge

Grace Coolidge

John Calvin Coolidge was the only president born on the fourth of July. He was born in Vermont on July 4, 1872. John, who was known by his middle name, Calvin, loved to learn at home from his mother, Victoria. He also attended school at the one room school house in his town. At age twelve, he went away to Black River Academy in Ludlow, Vermont.

Sadly, when Calvin was twelve years old, his mother died. Six years later, Calvin's sister, Abbie, died from appendicitis. Despite his great sadness, Calvin was still able to enjoy his life in Vermont, fishing and making maple syrup.

After completing school, Calvin went to Amherst College in Massachusetts, and he graduated in 1895. Eventually, Calvin moved to Massachusetts where he set up a place to work as a lawyer, called a **law firm**.

In 1899, Calvin decided to enter politics and became a state councilman in Northampton, Massachusetts. He helped to make decisions for the city of Northampton.

In 1905, Mr. Coolidge married a woman named Grace Goodhue, and they had two children together. Interestingly, Grace Coolidge was the first wife of a president to have graduated from a public university.

After getting married, Mr. Coolidge went on to hold many other government jobs in Massachusetts. Between 1906 and 1918, he was a state congressman, the mayor of Northampton, and a state senator for Massachusetts. In addition to these three political offices, Mr. Coolidge was also elected as the governor of Massachusetts in 1918.

Since he worked in the government for many years as a Republican, Mr. Coolidge was chosen as Warren Harding's vice presidential candidate in 1920, and they won the election.

A few years later, in 1923, President William Harding died while on a trip across the country. Mr. Coolidge was with his family in Vermont at the time and was **sworn in** immediately as president by his father, who was a government official. While he was president, Mr. Coolidge was known for being very quiet and not saying much at all. This is why he is known as "Silent Cal."

While Warren Harding was president, many scandals occurred. President Coolidge fired all of the people who had been sneaky and dishonest during Warren Harding's presidency.

Also, while he was president, Mr. Coolidge lowered taxes for many Americans and also for many businesses. As a result, businesses did not have to pay as much money to the government and began to thrive (do well).

In 1924, President Coolidge was reelected. He continued what he had been working on during his first term. He also worked to resolve problems that were going on with Mexico and Nicaragua.

After Mr. Coolidge's presidency ended, he went home to Vermont. While there, he wrote a book about his life called, The Autobiography of Calvin Coolidge.

In 1933, Calvin Coolidge died from a heart attack at age sixty.

Calvin Coolidge's second inauguration

Calvin Coolidge's childhood home in Vermont

REVIEW BITES

VOCABULARY

Law firm – A place where people practice law

Sworn in – When someone takes an oath and makes a promise to God to be honest and loyal in either what they say, or in their new job

FUN FACT

Calvin Coolidge had many pets, including a raccoon named Rebecca. President Coolidge would walk Rebecca around with a leash.

REVIEW QUESTIONS

1. What are some of the government jobs that Calvin Coolidge had?

2. Calvin Coolidge was the governor of which state?

3. Why did businesses do so well while Calvin Coolidge was president?

1. State councilman, mayor, state senator, governor, and vice president 2. Massachusetts 3. Mainly because taxes were lowered

31

Herbert Hoover
(1929-1933)

Herbert Hoover

Lou Hoover

Herbert Hoover was born in Iowa in 1874. His parents were **devout** Quakers, and Herbert learned many important life lessons from them. The Quakers were a religious society of people who believed in simple ways of living and worship. They were also devoted to peaceful principles.

When Herbert was very young, his father died, and three years after that, his mother died as well. This left Herbert and his siblings as **orphans**, and they went to live in Oregon with one of their uncles.

Even though he had grown up very poor, Herbert

eventually attended Stanford University. While in college, Herbert met a woman named Lou Henry. They got married a few years later in 1899, and they had two children together. Lou was an active woman during her life, and she led many clubs and groups.

After he graduated from college, Mr. Hoover went to work in gold mines, which are places where men dig for gold in caves or mountains. Since he did well in that job, Mr. Hoover became an **engineer** and inspected different mines to make sure they were safe. Because of this job, he and his wife, Lou, traveled all over the world, even to China. During this time, Mr. Hoover became very wealthy.

When World War I began in 1914, Mr. Hoover was living in London, England. He was given the important job of helping to evacuate American citizens from Europe. In 1917, he was offered his first U.S. government job. He accepted the offer, and President Woodrow Wilson put him in charge of an important organization called the U.S. Food Administration.

In addition to working for President Wilson, Mr. Hoover also worked for Presidents Harding and Coolidge. His job was to help manage and regulate American businesses as the U.S. secretary of commerce.

Interestingly, Mr. Hoover was never elected to a

government office until he was elected president in 1928. At that time, the Republicans were popular all across America, and Mr. Hoover won the election in a landslide.

In 1929, only a few months after he was elected, the stock market crashed. When people buy stocks in a company, they can earn money when those companies do well. Around this time, businesses were losing money, and some were even closing. Many Americans who had bought stocks in those companies lost all of their money and became very poor. To try and help, churches and private charities opened soup kitchens all over the country. People could go and get a free meal of hot soup and bread or coffee and a doughnut. This difficult financial time is known as "The Great Depression."

President Hoover did not think the government should get involved in the relief effort and instead, encouraged private groups to give money to help people. He also removed many of the fancy and expensive items from the White House. Many people unfairly blamed President Hoover for their financial troubles, even though it was not his fault.

In 1932, President Hoover ran for a second term but lost to Franklin D. Roosevelt. After his presidency, Mr. Hoover remained very active in helping people all over the world. When World War II began, he headed the Polish Relief Commission. Several years later, President Truman asked him to be in charge of the Food Supply for the World Famine organization. He also established the Hoover Library on War, Revolution, and Peace at Stanford University and served as the chairman of the Boys Clubs of America.

Herbert Hoover died in 1964 at ninety years old.

People in line at a soup kitchen during the Great Depression

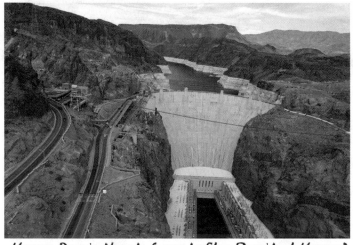

Hoover Dam in Nevada (named after President Hoover)

VOCABULARY

Devout – Deeply devoted to a religious way of life

Orphans – Children who do not have any parents

Engineer – Someone who designs machines or buildings

Depression – A time when businesses stop running and many people lose their jobs

FUN FACT

While living in the White House, Herbert Hoover's son had two pet alligators, and they would sometimes wander around the lawns.

REVIEW QUESTIONS

1. What job made Herbert Hoover very wealthy?

2. Herbert Hoover helped the Europeans during what two major wars?

3. During what difficult time was Herbert Hoover president?

1. Engineer 2. World War I and World War II
3. The Great Depression

Franklin D. Roosevelt

Eleanor Roosevelt

Franklin Delano Roosevelt (FDR) was born in Hyde Park, New York in January of 1882. Franklin grew up in a much wealthier lifestyle than many of the presidents before him. Franklin had many **tutors** who taught him at home. He learned how to speak Greek and Latin, and he loved to do outside activities. When he completed school, Franklin attended Harvard University.

One of Franklin's cousins was a girl named Eleanor. In 1905, Franklin and Eleanor got married, and they had six children together.

In 1911, Mr. Roosevelt began his career in politics when he was elected as a state senator in New York. Around this time, Mr. Roosevelt contracted a sickness called polio, which caused him to be paralyzed and have to use a wheelchair for the rest of his life.

In 1914, Mr. Roosevelt tried to obtain the nomination as the Democratic presidential candidate but failed. In 1920, he ran as the vice presidential candidate for Democratic nominee James Cox, but they lost the election to Warren Harding. Despite these losses, Mr. Roosevelt went on to become the governor of New York in 1929. Three years later, in 1932, Mr. Roosevelt ran for president as a Democrat and won.

During FDR's presidency, Mrs. Roosevelt kept very busy fulfilling her duties as first lady. She often spoke about different issues, such as civil rights, job equality, poverty, and child labor.

President Roosevelt tried to help Americans during the Great Depression. He formed a plan called the "New Deal," which gave government assistance to Americans. However, most of his plans did not actually help or improve America. The Supreme Court said that six of FDR's plans were unconstitutional, which meant that they went against the U.S. Constitution.

In 1936, Mr. Roosevelt was elected to a second term as president and continued with his "New Deal" plans. However, another large problem began during this time: World War II.

For many years, Germany was angry about losing World War I and the harsh terms forced upon them by the Allies in the Treaty of Versailles. Adolf Hitler, the German leader at that time, started to build up an army in Europe. In 1939, Hitler attacked Poland, and this started World War II. Germany, Italy, Russia, and Japan fought against Great Britain and France for the first few years of the war. However, Russia eventually switched sides and joined with Great Britain and France.

Even though America and Great Britain were allies (friends who work together), President Roosevelt kept America out of the war. He did, however, send some tanks and supplies to try and help Great Britain.

In 1940, President Roosevelt was elected to a third term, and this made him the first person to be elected more than two times. He was elected mainly because people were happy that he had kept them out of the war. However, on December 7, 1941, Japan attacked America in Pearl Harbor, Hawaii. Because of this, President Roosevelt decided to enter America into the war.

World War II continued for four more years. During that time, Mr. Roosevelt was elected as president a fourth time in 1944. However, President Roosevelt never completed his fourth term. He died on April 12, 1945 at age sixty-three, a few months before World War II ended. Vice president, Harry Truman, became the next president.

During Harry Truman's presidency, the 22nd amendment was added to the U.S. Constitution which said that a president could only serve two terms. Many people thought that President Roosevelt had been in power for too long.

Pearl Harbor Attack

Dime

My Great Grandpa, who served at Pearl Harbor

REVIEW BITES

VOCABULARY

Tutor – A person who teaches someone else privately

Issues – Problems or concerns

FUN FACT

President Franklin D. Roosevelt had a dog named Fala. Fala became so popular while Mr. Roosevelt was president that people would cut hairs off of him as a souvenir.

REVIEW QUESTIONS

1. Franklin Roosevelt served as the governor of which state?

2. Franklin Roosevelt was the president of America during what war?

3. How many times was Franklin Roosevelt elected as president?

33

Harry S. Truman
(1945-1953)

Harry S. Truman

Bess Truman

Harry S. Truman was born in Missouri in 1884.
The letter "S" in his name does not actually stand for
anything. Harry's parents could not decide on a middle
name for him, so they just put "S."

Harry grew up with poor eyesight and had to wear
big glasses. Harry loved school, reading, and playing the
piano. Once he finished school, Harry tried to get into a
military academy called West Point, but because of his
poor eyesight, they would not let him in.

Instead of going to the academy, Harry decided

to work for a while. He worked at a railroad, a newspaper shop, a construction business, and a bank. After he had worked at these jobs for a while, Harry decided to join the U.S. Army in 1905.

When America entered World War I in 1917, Harry was part of a group called the 129th Field Artillery. During the war, Harry eventually became a **captain**.

In 1919, after he had come home from the war, Harry married a woman named Elizabeth ("Bess") Wallace, whom he had known since he was six years old. They had one child together.

In 1922, Mr. Truman was elected as a **judge** on the Jackson County Court in Missouri. Several years later, in 1934, he was elected as a U.S. Senator. He continued working as a Senator for ten years until 1945.

When Franklin D. Roosevelt ran for president a fourth time in 1944, he chose Mr. Truman as his vice presidential candidate, and they won the election. A few months later, in 1945, President Roosevelt died, which made Mr. Truman the next president.

Throughout Mr. Truman's presidency, America was involved in three major wars: World War II, the Cold War, and the Korean War. World War II was almost over when

Mr. Truman became president. Even though Germany had surrendered, Japan had not. Because of this, President Truman had U.S. pilots drop two atomic bombs on cities in Japan. Sadly, these bombs killed hundreds of thousands of people. As a result, Japan surrendered, and World War II finally ended. President Truman sent money to non-communist European countries, like West Germany, to help relieve them from the distress of famine after World War II.

The Cold War began after World War II. No battles were actually fought during this war. America and Russia tried to convince other countries to have the same kind of government that they had. President Truman encouraged countries to have a free, democratic government while Russia was trying to have countries become communist nations. (Communism takes away people's rights and freedoms.)

In 1948, Mr. Truman was elected as president for a second term. During this time, the Korean War began in 1950. This war was fought between America and Russia in a country called Korea. America fought so that Korea could have a free and democratic government, and Russia fought to try and make Korea a communist nation. The fighting continued until after President Truman's second term. Eventually, in 1953, America and Russia agreed to a ceasefire, which meant that they decided to end the fighting. However, this left Korea divided into two countries, with Russia controlling the North and America controlling the South. North Korea is still a communist country today while South Korea is democratic.

In 1953, after his presidency ended, Harry Truman went back home to Missouri. He wrote three books, entitled, <u>Years of Decisions</u>, <u>Years of Trial and Hope</u>, and <u>Mr. Citizen</u>.

Harry Truman died in December of 1972 at the age of eighty-eight.

Harry S. Truman during World War I

Atomic bomb

REVIEW BITES

VOCABULARY

Military academy – A school that trains military officers

Captain – A type of leader in the military, who commands a certain number of soldiers

Judge – Someone who makes decisions in a court based on the law

FUN FACT

By the time he was fifteen years old, Harry Truman had read ALL of the books in his home town library.

REVIEW QUESTIONS

1. Harry Truman fought in what war?

2. For whom did Harry Truman serve
   as vice president?

3. Name one of the wars that occurred while
   Harry Truman was president.

34

Dwight D. Eisenhower (1953-1961)

Dwight D. Eisenhower

Mamie Eisenhower

David Dwight Eisenhower was born in Denison, Texas on October 14, 1890. Even though his first name was David, he was known as Dwight D. Eisenhower for most of his life. Dwight lived in a tiny house in Texas with his parents and five brothers. When Dwight was still young, his family moved to Kansas, which is where he grew up.

When Dwight got older, he had different jobs, such as cooking and washing dishes, to help provide for his family. Dwight also loved to play sports, especially football. Eventually, he went on to a military academy called West Point and played football there. Dwight graduated from West Point in 1915, and one year later, he married a woman named Marie Doud ("Mamie"). They had two children together.

During World War I, Mr. Eisenhower served in the military as an Army captain and was quickly promoted to major. His job was to train men on how to be soldiers. Even though he did not get to fight himself, Mr. Eisenhower knew that his job was very important.

Between World War I and World War II, Mr. Eisenhower held many important positions in the military, including **Chief of Staff** for the Army. In 1941, when America entered into World War II, Mr. Eisenhower had become a **colonel** and was in charge of many men. He made some extremely important decisions during World War II about the strategies America should use to fight against Germany and its allies.

Mr. Eisenhower eventually became an Army general and came up with the military plans for "D-Day." This was a very significant event in World War II. On D-Day, June 6, 1944, America and Great Britain captured the Normandy Beaches in France. From there, they took back a lot of land in Europe from the Germans that had been lost during the war. Because his plan worked so well, General Eisenhower became very popular with the American people.

Once World War II ended in 1945, Mr. Eisenhower returned to America as a hero. He had become a five-star general, which is the highest rank/position you can earn in the military.

For the next seven years, Mr. Eisenhower held some important positions. He became the president of Columbia University and also the main commander of the U.S. Army in America and Europe.

Since he had become so popular with the American people, Mr. Eisenhower decided to run for president. In 1952, he ran as a Republican, and while campaigning, his slogan was "I like Ike." "Ike" had been his nickname since his childhood. Mr. Eisenhower won the election in a landslide.

Soon after he became president, Mr. Eisenhower helped to end the Korean War. He also set up NASA (National Aeronautics and Space Administration). NASA eventually helped to send Americans into space. They did this so that they could beat the Russians in the "Space Race." (see section 35)

During his presidency, Mr. Eisenhower worked to stop America's debt from getting larger. The U.S.

Highway System was also created, which provided safer and better roads for all Americans. President Eisenhower also worked to end segregation in America. Segregation was when black people were treated unfairly compared to white people.

In 1961, after his presidency ended, Mr. Eisenhower moved to Gettysburg, Pennsylvania with his wife, Mamie. He spent his time golfing and writing, and published a few books, including one about his time in the White House.

Dwight Eisenhower died on March 28, 1969, in Washington, D.C. at age seventy-eight.

General Eisenhower talking to D-Day soldiers

Dwight D. Eisenhower playing golf

President Eisenhower's home in Gettysburg, Pennsylvania

REVIEW BITES

VOCABULARY

Chief of Staff – A person in charge of a group, organization, or branch of the military

Colonel – A type of leader in the military, who commands a certain number of soldiers

Landslide – When a person wins an election by a large number of votes

FUN FACT

In 1955, during Dwight Eisenhower's presidency, Disneyland opened in Anaheim, California.

REVIEW QUESTIONS

1. Dwight Eisenhower played football at what military academy?

2. During World War II, what was the day called in which America and Great Britain captured the Normandy Beaches in France?

3. While he was president, what system of roads did Dwight Eisenhower create?

35

John F. Kennedy
(1961–1963)

John F. Kennedy

Jacqueline Kennedy

John F. Kennedy (JFK) was born in Massachusetts on May 29, 1917. As a child, John was often very sick with colitis and also suffered from back problems.

Once he finished school, John attended the London School of Economics, Princeton University, and Harvard University. While at Harvard, John studied politics and graduated in 1940.

When America entered World War II in 1941, Mr. Kennedy joined the U.S. Navy. One time during the war, he was in command of a boat called a PT-109 when the

Japanese destroyed his ship by smashing into it with a huge warship. Although some of the men on board died, Mr. Kennedy helped save some of the surviving crew. This made him a war hero, and as a result, he received two awards: the Purple Heart and the Marine Corps Medal.

In 1946, Mr. Kennedy was elected into the U.S. House of Representatives. He worked there for seven years and was later elected into the U.S. Senate in 1953. That same year, Mr. Kennedy married a young woman named Jacqueline Bouvier. They had four children together, but sadly, two of them died young.

In 1960, Mr. Kennedy ran for president as a Democrat against Richard Nixon. He won the election by a very small margin.

While her husband was president, Mrs. Kennedy began restoring and redecorating the White House. She had antiques, collectibles, furniture, and artwork all brought in to remodel the house.

During Mr. Kennedy's presidency, America and Russia were involved in a space "race" to see who could accomplish things in space first. President Kennedy worked hard to motivate America to put an astronaut on the moon before 1970. They succeeded and won the space race in 1969 when Neil Armstrong, an American astronaut, became the first man to walk on the moon.

During this same time, America had many problems with a country called Cuba. America tried to help the Cubans get rid of their communist leader, Fidel Castro, but their plan failed. Russia, another communist nation, began sending **missiles** to Cuba. Since Cuba is located so close to the United States, people were worried that Cuba would shoot the missiles at America. President Kennedy made agreements with Russian leader Nikita Khrushchev to remove the missiles from Cuba. This is known as the "Cuban Missile Crisis."

President Kennedy also worked to end segregation in America, which was when black people were treated unfairly compared to white people. During this time, a man named Martin Luther King Jr. was working hard to peacefully protest against segregation and help black people achieve equal rights.

In 1963, President Kennedy started to **campaign** for his second term as president. While campaigning in Dallas, President Kennedy was riding in a car in a parade with his wife, Jacqueline, and the governor of Texas and his wife. During the parade, a man named Lee Harvey Oswald shot President Kennedy. They rushed the president to a local hospital, but sadly, he died only an hour later on November 22, 1963. Immediately, his vice president, Lyndon B. Johnson, became president. Mr. Oswald was caught and charged with the crime but was murdered before the trial by a man named Jacob Rubenstein ("Jack Ruby").

After President Kennedy died, there was a huge **funeral** for him in Washington, D.C. Ever since then, there has been a flame burning continuously for him at his gravesite in Arlington National Cemetery in Washington, D.C. It is Known as "The Eternal Flame."

Half-dollar coin

Martin Luther King Jr. giving his "I Have a Dream" speech

The Eternal Flame

REVIEW BITES

VOCABULARY

Missiles – Small rockets that can do a lot of damage

Campaign (verb) – An organized effort to get someone elected to a political position

Funeral – A ceremony that is performed after someone dies

FUN FACT

John F. Kennedy was the youngest person to be elected as president at age forty-three. He was also the only American president to practice the Roman Catholic religion.

☆☆☆☆☆☆☆☆☆☆☆☆

REVIEW QUESTIONS

1. During what war did the Japanese destroy John F. Kennedy's boat?

2. While John F. Kennedy was president, what event took place in which Russia sent missiles to the country of Cuba?

3. What major event did President Kennedy hope to accomplish by 1970?

3. To have an American land on the moon
1. World War II 2. The Cuban Missile Crisis

36

Lyndon B. Johnson
(1963-1969)

Lyndon B. Johnson

Lady Bird Johnson

Lyndon Baines Johnson was born in Johnson City, Texas on August 27, 1908. He had three sisters and one brother. Lyndon did well in school and loved to debate other people. During his teenage years, Lyndon had a job as a **shoe shiner** to help provide money for his family.

After high school, Lyndon went to Southwest Texas State Teachers College, and during college, he got a job as a teacher. He graduated from college in 1930 and continued to teach.

In 1935, Lyndon married a young woman named

Claudia Taylor ("Lady Bird"). They had two children together. When Mr. Johnson became the president of America, "Lady Bird" gave many speeches to try and help advance different causes.

In 1937, Mr. Johnson began his work in the United States Congress when he was elected into the House of Representatives. He was there until 1941 and then went to Australia to fight in World War II. He served in the U.S. Navy, and he earned an award called the Silver Star.

When he came home from the war, he returned to his job as a Representative. In 1948, Mr. Johnson was elected into the U.S. Senate and became an important leader there.

Since so many people in the southern states supported Mr. Johnson, John F. Kennedy (JFK) asked him to be his vice presidential candidate in 1960. Mr. Johnson agreed, and in 1961, Mr. Kennedy won the election. Sadly, in 1963, President Kennedy was killed in Dallas, Texas. Because of this, Mr. Johnson became the next president of America that same day.

During his presidency, Mr. Johnson developed a plan to help everyone get treated fairly throughout America. He called this plan the "Great Society." It was similar to the "New Deal" of Franklin D. Roosevelt. In 1964, President Johnson also signed a law called the Civil Rights Act, which made it illegal to practice segregation in America. Because of his work to help black people, President Johnson became very popular with some Americans and won a landslide victory in 1964 for a second term as president.

Throughout his second term, President Johnson had to lead the country through the Vietnam War. This war started when communists in North Vietnam attacked South Vietnam. They did this so that they could take over all of Vietnam and control its government. In 1964, President Johnson sent American soldiers to help South Vietnam for many years. Unfortunately, the Vietnam War and race riots across the country made many Americans angry with President Johnson, and he chose not to run for president again in 1968.

In 1969, Mr. Johnson went back home to Texas. He enjoyed three years of retirement before he died in January of 1973 at age sixty-four.

Vietnam War helicopter

President Johnson signing the Civil Rights Act of 1964

REVIEW BITES

VOCABULARY

Shoe shiner – Someone who cleans and shines shoes

Retirement – The time someone spends once they have finished their life work

FUN FACT

Lyndon Johnson owned many dogs throughout his life. One of his dogs was named Yuki. Sometimes, President Johnson would entertain his guests by singing while Yuki howled.

☆☆☆☆☆☆☆☆☆☆

REVIEW QUESTIONS

1. What job did Lyndon Johnson have during and after college?

2. For whom did Lyndon Johnson serve as vice president?

3. What law did President Johnson sign that gave black people equal treatment throughout America?

1. Teacher 2. President John F. Kennedy
3. The Civil Rights Act of 1964

Richard M. Nixon

Pat Nixon

    Richard Milhous Nixon was born in California in 1913. Richard's father owned a gas station, and Richard sometimes worked there.

    After Richard finished high school, he received a **scholarship** from Harvard University. However, since his family could not pay the difference to send him there, he went to Whittier College instead where he studied history. From there, Richard went to Duke University to study law, and he graduated college in 1937.

    In 1940, Richard married a young woman named

Thelma Ryan, who was called "Pat." They had two children together.

In 1942, Mr. Nixon joined the U.S. Navy and fought in World War II. When he returned home from the war, he was elected into the U.S. House of Representatives. In 1950, he was elected into the U.S. Senate. Throughout his campaign for **Congress**, Mr. Nixon tried to discredit his opponent. As a result, he was referred to as "Tricky Dick" in a 1950 newspaper ad paid for by Democrats. The newspaper writers were urging Americans to look into "Tricky Dick" Nixon's Republican record. (It is a common misconception that this nickname came from the Watergate scandal, but it actually started decades before that.)

In 1952, when Dwight D. Eisenhower ran for president, he chose Mr. Nixon as his vice presidential candidate. Together, they served two consecutive terms for a total of eight years. In 1960, Mr. Nixon decided to run for president but lost to John F. Kennedy. Two years later, Mr. Nixon ran for governor of California but lost. Finally, in 1968, when Mr. Nixon ran for president again, he won.

Throughout his presidency, Mr. Nixon encountered

many problems because of the Vietnam War. Even though he wanted America to keep helping South Vietnam, President Nixon eventually removed all of the American soldiers from Vietnam in 1973.

One of President Nixon's achievements was making peace with China. For many years, America and China did not have a good relationship with each other and did not get along well. However, in 1972, President Nixon visited China and worked out peace agreements with the Chinese leader at that time, Chou En-Lai.

Unfortunately, despite some of his achievements, President Nixon is most often remembered for a scandal. In 1972, some men broke into a place called the Watergate Complex in Washington, D.C. where many Democratic politicians met to discuss important things. Some of President Nixon's advisors had paid the men to break in so they could record secret information that might help the president. However, in 1974, Americans discovered what the men had done. Sadly, President Nixon lied to Congress about the timing of the break-in, and people wanted to impeach him because of it. Instead of being impeached, President Nixon **resigned** instead in 1974. This whole affair is known as the Watergate scandal.

After his resignation, Richard Nixon wrote four books, including one called, <u>The Real War</u>.

Mr. Nixon died in 1994 in New York City at the age of eighty-one.

Charles (Chuck) Colson
(see "Fun Fact" on next page)

The Watergate Complex

REVIEW BITES

VOCABULARY

Scholarship – When a group or foundation gives a gift of money to someone to help pay for their education

Congress – The place where decisions are made concerning America's laws; it is divided into the U.S. Senate and the U.S. House of Representatives

Resigned – Gave up a job

FUN FACT

During the Watergate Scandal, one of President Nixon's advisors was Charles Colson. Because of the scandal, Mr. Colson went to jail. However, he had become a Christian before going to prison, and after leaving jail, he founded a ministry called Prison Fellowship.

REVIEW QUESTIONS

1. For whom did Richard Nixon serve as vice president?

2. President Nixon removed American soldiers from what country?

3. While Richard Nixon was president, what was the name of the scandal that led to his resignation?

Gerald R. Ford

Betty Ford

Leslie King was born in Nebraska on July 14, 1913. While he was still a baby, Leslie's parents divorced. His mother, Dorothy, married another man named Gerald Ford. Dorothy renamed Leslie as Gerald Rudolph Ford, after his new stepfather. Gerald did not know that his stepfather was not his biological father until many years later.

While growing up, Gerald loved to play football. He was also a boy scout for many years. In the 1930s, Gerald went to college at the University of Michigan where he learned about government and other subjects. He loved playing football and considered making it his career but went to Yale University Law School instead. He graduated from Yale in 1941.

In 1942, Gerald joined the U.S. Navy and fought in World War II. He participated in many battles on islands in the Pacific Ocean. After the war ended, Gerald received many different awards called battle stars.

A few years after he had come home from the war, Gerald met a woman named Elizabeth Bloomer Warren, also known as "Betty." Gerald and Betty were married in 1948, and they had four children together. That same year, Mr. Ford was elected into his first government position in the U.S. House of Representatives. He worked there for more than twenty years.

In 1973, President Richard Nixon's vice president, Spiro Agnew, resigned because he knew he was going to get in trouble for some bad decisions he had made. So, President Nixon chose Mr. Ford as his new vice president. Then, when President Nixon resigned in 1974, Mr. Ford became America's thirty-eighth president.

Because of President Nixon's lies, Americans did not trust the government as much as they had before. President Ford tried to earn back the trust of the

American people. Thankfully, many people began to have faith in the government again. Interestingly, President Ford ended up **pardoning** Richard Nixon for his lies, which angered many Americans. President Ford had done it so that the country could move on after what had happened with the Watergate scandal.

During his presidency, Mr. Ford tried to help the U.S. **economy** by preventing the government from spending too much money. In addition to reducing government spending, President Ford also began a new program called WIN (Whip Inflation Now). This program was designed to lower inflation, which is when money loses some of its value. He also helped thousands of Americans and Vietnamese people escape from Vietnam before the communist North Vietnamese leaders took over.

In 1976, Mr. Ford ran for president but lost to Jimmy Carter. After his presidency, he continued to remain active, earning the Presidential Medal of Freedom and other awards.

Gerald Ford died on December 26, 2006, at the age of ninety-three.

Young Gerald Ford playing football

President Ford pardoning Richard Nixon

REVIEW BITES

VOCABULARY

Pardon – To forgive or excuse an error or offense

Economy – The amount of goods and services a country produces and consumes

FUN FACT

While playing football, Gerald Ford did so well that an NFL football team called the Green Bay Packers wanted him to be on their team.

REVIEW QUESTIONS

1. What sport did Gerald Ford love to play?

2. What was the first government office that Gerald Ford held?

3. Gerald Ford became the president after who resigned?

Jimmy Carter
(1977-1981)

Jimmy Carter

Rosalynn Carter

James Earl Carter Jr. was born in Georgia in 1924. James was (and still is) known as "Jimmy." Jimmy's father owned a peanut farm in Georgia. Sometimes, Jimmy would work for his father selling peanuts on the side of the road in Plains, Georgia.

Growing up, Jimmy went to a school where black children were not allowed to attend. However, some of Jimmy's friends were black.

Once he finished high school, Jimmy studied at two different colleges. First, he attended Southwestern

Junior College and then studied math and physics at Georgia Tech University.

Jimmy finished college in 1943 and went to the U.S. Naval Academy. After graduating from the academy, Jimmy went to work on two U.S. naval ships. While in the Navy, Jimmy married a young woman named Eleanor Smith, who is known by her middle name, Rosalynn. They had four children together.

When his father died, Jimmy retired from the Navy and came home to run his father's peanut business. Several years later, in 1962, he was elected to his first government office as a **state senator** in Georgia. In 1970, he was elected governor of Georgia.

In 1976, the Democrats chose Mr. Carter as their candidate for president. Because most people did not know who he was, he worked hard to make himself known by giving several speeches and meeting new people all across America. Later that same year, he was elected president.

During his presidency, many Americans lost their jobs and inflation increased. Inflation is when money becomes less valuable, which makes people have to pay more for things like groceries and gasoline. To be a good example during this time, President Carter decided to sell his limousine and **yacht** because he thought that he should live more like ordinary Americans.

During this time, President Carter worked to try and solve race relations in America. He also tried to create peace between countries in Europe, Asia, Africa, and the Middle East. In one example, he came up with a plan called the Camp David Accords, which helped to make peace between Israel and Egypt. Sadly, during this same time, a group of Islamic terrorists took over the U.S. Embassy in Iran and captured fifty-two Americans because they were angry about a decision President Carter had made. The American hostages were held as prisoners for 444 days. This is known as the Iranian Hostage Crisis. Thankfully, the Americans were eventually set free in 1981, just minutes after Jimmy Carter's presidency ended, while President Reagan was giving his inaugural speech.

After losing the 1980 election to Ronald Reagan, Mr. Carter went back home to Georgia. Since then, he has written several books, including one about his time as president. Mr. Carter has also continued working to try and bring peace throughout the world. Because of this, he won an award called the Nobel Peace Prize in 2002.

Jimmy Carter currently lives in Georgia with his wife, Rosalynn.

Jimmy Carter on his peanut farm in Georgia

President Carter with Israeli and Egyptian leaders

Some of the American hostages coming home soon after President Reagan's inauguration

REVIEW BITES

VOCABULARY

State Senator – A member of a state's senate

Yacht – A large, fancy, and expensive boat

FUN FACT

Jimmy Carter can read over 2,000 words a minute. That is equivalent to reading the first four sections of this book in sixty seconds.

REVIEW QUESTIONS

1. What kind of farm did Jimmy Carter's father own?

2. In which branch of the military did Jimmy Carter serve?

3. What were the agreements called that President Carter made with Israel and Egypt?

40 Ronald Reagan (1981-1989)

Ronald Reagan

Nancy Reagan

Ronald Wilson Reagan was born in Tampico, Illinois on February 6, 1911. Throughout his childhood, Ronald was known as "Dutch" because his father said that he looked like a "fat little Dutchman" when he was born. Throughout his childhood in the 1920s, Ronald and his family suffered during the Great Depression.

After high school, Ronald attended Eureka College and was the leader of many different groups, including the swim team. After college, he became a sports **broadcaster** and was a radio announcer for many different sporting events.

In 1937, Mr. Reagan decided to become an actor. He

moved to Hollywood, California and began his acting career. He was the star (main character) in over fifty movies. One of his most famous movies is called *Knute Rockne: All American.* In this movie, Mr. Reagan played a football player called "the Gipper," which ended up becoming one of his most famous nicknames.

In 1940, Mr. Reagan married an **actress** named Jane Wyman. They had one child together and also adopted a second child. However, they divorced in 1948. In 1952, Mr. Reagan married another actress named Nancy Davis, and they had two children together.

During World War II, Mr. Reagan took a break from Hollywood to serve in the U.S. Army. Even though he could not fight because of his poor eyesight, he stayed back in America to make training movies for the Army.

In 1964, a Republican named Barry Goldwater ran for president. Mr. Reagan gave many speeches to help him get elected, but Mr. Goldwater lost. However, these speeches made Mr. Reagan more well known throughout the country.

In 1966, Mr. Reagan was elected as governor of California and served eight years in this position. In 1976, he ran for president but lost the Republican nomination. However, four years later, in 1980, Mr. Reagan ran again, and this time, he won the election.

A few months after he was elected, President Reagan

was shot by a man named John Hinckley Jr. Thankfully, President Reagan survived and recovered in a few weeks.

Throughout his presidency, Mr. Reagan worked hard to improve the U.S. economy. His economic plan gave jobs to 16 million people and was later referred to as "Reaganomics." President Reagan also lowered taxes for many Americans.

In 1984, President Reagan ran for a second term and won every state except Minnesota. In the largest election landslide victory in history, President Reagan won the most **electoral college** votes in any presidential election (525 out of a possible 538).

During his second term in office, President Reagan worked to make America's military stronger and also made agreements with Russia to help end the Cold War. President Reagan worked with Russian leader Mikhail Gorbachev to eliminate many dangerous weapons called missiles.

Around this time, some of President Reagan's advisors had made secret deals with a country called Iran, in which they agreed to sell the Iranians powerful weapons in exchange for the release of some American hostages. The Americans were taken captive by Islamic terrorists and held as prisoners in a country called Lebanon. However, Marine Lieutenant Colonel Oliver North, along with some other government officials, secretly sent the money from the sale of the weapons to Iran, to rebel fighters in Nicaragua instead of to the U.S. government. These fighters in Nicaragua were known as "contras." Lieutenant Colonel North did this in order to help the "contras" fight against the communist government in Nicaragua. President Reagan said that he did not know that money had been sent to the "contras" and apologized for the scandal. In 1993, a government court confirmed that President Reagan had told the truth when he said he hadn't known about Colonel North sending the money. This whole ordeal is known as the Iran-Contra Affair.

In 1989, after his presidency ended, Mr. Reagan went home to his ranch in California. Sadly, he suffered from a disease called Alzheimer's for nine years.

Ronald Reagan died of pneumonia on June 5, 2004, at age ninety-three.

Lieutenant Colonel Oliver North
testifying before Congress

Ronald Reagan as
"the Gipper" in the film,
Knute Rockne: All American

Mikhail Gorbachev and President Reagan

REVIEW BITES

VOCABULARY

Broadcaster – Someone who announces things on the radio or television

Actress – A female actor

Electoral College – A system which gives a person who is running for president a certain number of votes from each state that he/she wins

Ranch – A home on a large piece of land where crops and/or animals are raised

FUN FACT

Ronald Reagan loved jelly beans. When he became president, he bought over 6,000 pounds of blueberry-flavored jelly beans.

☆☆☆☆☆☆☆☆☆☆☆☆

REVIEW QUESTIONS

1. Before he became president, what career did Ronald Reagan have in Hollywood?

2. Ronald Reagan was the governor of which state?

3. During his presidency, what was Ronald Reagan's plan called that helped improve the U.S. economy?

1. Actor 2. California 3. "Reaganomics"

41 George H. W. Bush (1989-1993)

George H. W. Bush

Barbara Bush

George Hebert Walker Bush was born in Massachusetts in 1924. He grew up in Connecticut with four siblings. As a young boy, he attended different **private schools**. After graduating high school at eighteen years old, George joined the U.S. Navy and served as the youngest pilot in World War II. Amazingly, George flew fifty-eight combat missions and was shot down four times. After the war, he earned a medal called the Distinguished Flying Cross.

In 1945, before the end of World War II, George came home on furlough (vacation). In 1946, he married

Barbara Pierce, and they had six children together. Sadly, one of their daughters, Robin, died of leukemia at age four. Later in life, one of their sons, George W. Bush, was elected governor of Texas and went on to become America's forty-third president in 2001. Also, their son, Jeb, became the governor of Florida. He ran for president in 2016 but did not win the Republican nomination.

After World War II, George attended Yale University. After graduation, he worked as a businessman in the oil industry and became very wealthy.

In 1966, Mr. Bush was elected into the U.S. House of Representatives but only after he lost an election to become a Senator. A few years later, President Richard Nixon appointed Mr. Bush to be a U.S. ambassador to the United Nations (UN). The UN was formed in 1945 and is an organization comprised of many different countries. The ambassadors from each country meet to discuss different issues going on around the world and try to help each other achieve and maintain peace. Mr. Bush's job was to try and help solve America's problems with other countries in hopes of finding peaceful resolutions.

In 1976, Mr. Bush became the **director** of the Central Intelligence Agency (CIA). The CIA is a federal government agency responsible for providing national security to America. They gather secret security information from around the world and then provide the information to the president and his Cabinet so they can best determine how to help protect America from enemy attacks.

In 1980, Mr. Bush ran for president as a Republican but lost the nomination to Ronald Reagan. When Mr. Reagan was campaigning, he asked Mr. Bush to be his vice presidential candidate. Mr. Bush accepted, Mr. Reagan won the election, and they served two consecutive terms together. When President Reagan was shot in 1981 and had to go to the hospital, Vice President Bush temporarily served as president for a few hours.

In 1989, after President Reagan's two terms ended, Mr. Bush ran for president and won in a landslide victory. During his presidency, he worked to help America have better relationships with other countries. One specific incident involved the country of Iraq attacking the small country of Kuwait. Iraq's leader, Saddam Hussein, wanted Kuwait's oil to help fund his military. President Bush worked with other countries to push Saddam Hussein back into Iraq. This war was called the Persian Gulf War and only lasted a few months. Because of this quick victory, President Bush became very popular with many Americans.

Also, in 1989, the Berlin Wall was torn down. The Berlin Wall was built by communists to separate West and East Germany. In 1991, the Soviet Union's communist government collapsed after almost fifty years. Both of these events are significant because they helped to end communism in many parts of the world.

Despite his many accomplishments, President Bush is remembered by some people for a negative reason. While campaigning for president, one of his promises was that he would not raise taxes. In one speech, he specifically said, "Read my lips. No new taxes." However, because the U.S. economy was not doing well, President Bush ended up having to increase taxes. By doing this, he broke his campaign promise, which made him unpopular with many Americans.

After his presidency ended, Mr. Bush and his wife moved back to Texas, and they still live there today.

President Ronald Reagan
with Vice President Bush

George H. W. Bush
as a Navy pilot

U.S. F-14A Tomcat fighter planes
during the Persian Gulf War

REVIEW BITES

VOCABULARY

Private schools – Schools that do not get money from the government and are paid for with tuition

Director – A person in charge of an activity, department, or organization

Nomination – When someone is selected to run for a government office

FUN FACT

George H. W. Bush does not like broccoli. While he was president, he said, "I am the president of the United States, and I am not going to eat any more broccoli!"

REVIEW QUESTIONS

1. During World War II, George Bush was the youngest pilot in which branch of the military?

2. Before he became president, George Bush was the director of what organization?

3. What war took place while George Bush was president?

Bill Clinton
(1993-2001)

Bill Clinton

Hillary Clinton

William Jefferson Blythe was born in Arkansas on August 19, 1946. His father died a few months before William was born. Several years later, William's mother, Virginia, married another man named Roger Clinton. Because of that, William changed his last name from "Blythe" to "Clinton." Also, his nickname was "Bill," and he was called that for the rest of his life.

After high school, Bill attended a few different colleges including Georgetown University and Oxford University, which is in England.

In 1974, after graduating from the University of Arkansas, Bill tried to get elected as a U.S. Representative but lost. While at college, Bill met a woman named Hillary Rodham. In 1975, they got married and had one child together. Mrs. Clinton went on to become a U.S. Senator and the secretary of state for President Barack Obama. She also ran for president in 2008 and 2016 but lost both times.

In 1978, at the age of thirty-two, Mr. Clinton was elected governor of Arkansas, which made him the youngest person to ever be elected as a governor in America. While governor, Mr. Clinton was involved in two **scandals**. One was called Whitewater and the other was called Trooper-Gate.

In 1992, Mr. Clinton ran for president as a Democrat and won. While president, Mr. Clinton worked to make **healthcare** better for people. However, many of his plans did not get passed into law. President Clinton also worked to stop the government from spending so much money. He worked to create more jobs and pay off some of America's debt. Interestingly, even though he was a Democrat, President Clinton sometimes agreed with Republicans on some issues.

During his presidency, two government shutdowns occurred. A government shutdown is when the members of Congress cannot come to a decision on something and certain government work stops for a little while. These particular shutdowns occurred because Republicans in Congress could not come to an agreement with President Clinton and the Democrats.

In 1996, President Clinton was reelected to a second term. During his second term, Mr. Clinton became involved in a serious scandal. Mr. Clinton had been doing inappropriate things with a woman named Monica Lewinsky. Sadly, President Clinton lied about it and said that he had not done anything wrong. Because of his lies, the U.S. House of Representatives voted to **impeach** him. Presidents Clinton and Andrew Johnson (see section 17) are the only American presidents to have been impeached. However, just like with President Andrew Johnson, the U.S. Senate did not vote to remove President Clinton from office, which meant he was able to finish his term.

In 2001, Mr. Clinton's presidency ended, and he went back home to Arkansas. He tried to help his wife, Hillary, get elected as president two times but was unsuccessful. President and Mrs. Clinton also started an organization called the Clinton Foundation. They have been accused of using a lot of the money that people give to the foundation for their own personal gain.

Mr. and Mrs. Clinton eventually left Arkansas and moved to New York, which is where they still live today.

Young Bill Clinton with President John F. Kennedy

President Clinton speaking about the Lewinsky scandal

REVIEW BITES

VOCABULARY

Scandal – Something that brings disgrace (embarrassment) to someone famous

Healthcare – Programs created by the government to give people money for their health insurance

Impeach – To remove a public official from his/her office

FUN FACT

As a teenager, Bill Clinton ran for so many high school student government offices that his principal did not allow him to run for any more.

REVIEW QUESTIONS

1. Bill Clinton was the governor of which state?

2. What did President Clinton work to improve for Americans?

3. Presidents Clinton and Andrew Johnson are the only two presidents to have been what?

1. Arkansas 2. Healthcare 3. Impeached

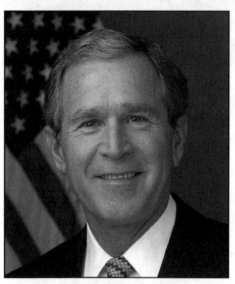

George W. Bush

Laura Bush

George Walker Bush was born in Connecticut on July 6, 1946. George's father, George H. W. Bush, was the forty-first president of America. This made them the second father and son pair to each become president. The first pair was John Adams and his son, John Quincy Adams.

George's family moved to Texas when he was young. He loved to play sports in school and wanted to become a professional baseball player. However, he decided to attend Yale University, just like his father had.

In 1968, George graduated from Yale University and joined the Texas Air **National Guard**. He learned how to fly planes, such as the F-102. In 1974, after completing his time in the National Guard, George returned home to Texas and became part-owner of a baseball team called the Texas Rangers.

In 1981, George married a woman named Laura Welch, after meeting her a few years before. They had two children together. While Mr. Bush was president, Mrs. Bush created programs that helped more American children learn how to read.

In 1988, when his father, George H. W. Bush, ran for president, Mr. Bush helped him by organizing his campaign. A few years later, in 1994, he ran for governor of Texas and won. Many Americans thought that George W. Bush was the most well-liked governor of a large state.

In 2000, George W. Bush ran for president as a Republican against Al Gore. Mr. Gore had been President Clinton's vice president. The election was very close, but George W. Bush won by a small margin.

As soon as he became president, Mr. Bush worked to lower **taxes**. In fact, in 2002, President Bush lowered taxes more than any other previous president.

Sadly, some very bad things happened during the first year of Mr. Bush's presidency. On September 11, 2001, a group of Islamic **terrorists** hijacked four American airplanes. The terrorists crashed two of the planes into the Twin Towers in New York City. More terrorists then crashed another plane into a building in Washington, D.C. called the Pentagon. Some more terrorists had taken over a fourth plane, but some very brave people on the plane tried to stop them. Sadly, the plane crashed into a field in Pennsylvania and everyone on board died.

After these tragic attacks, President Bush gave an important speech at the site in New York City (called "Ground Zero") to try and comfort the American people. He also sent American soldiers to a country called Iraq to try and stop the terrorists from attacking again. This started the Iraq War.

Since he helped to defend Americans from more terrorist attacks, and also because many Americans liked him, Mr. Bush was elected to a second term as president in 2004. President Bush continued to help fight the terrorists and also worked to keep the economy strong.

After his presidency ended in 2009, George W. Bush returned home to Texas with his wife, Laura, where they still live today.

George W. Bush, in the National Guard,
standing with his father, George H. W. Bush

World Trade Center Towers in New York City,
before the 9/11 attack

President Bush addressing the people at "Ground Zero"

REVIEW BITES

VOCABULARY

National Guard – A group of military reserves of the United States Armed Forces from each state

Taxes – Money that people have to pay to the government

Terrorists – People who do things to purposely hurt or scare other people

FUN FACT

George W. Bush loves baseball and owns 250 baseballs that were signed by famous players. He also loves to paint.

REVIEW QUESTIONS

1. Who was George W. Bush's father?

2. George W. Bush was the governor of which state?

3. On what day did terrorists attack the Twin Towers in New York City?

1. George H. W. Bush, the forty-first president of America
2. Texas 3. September 11, 2001

Barack Obama

Michelle Obama

Barack Obama was born in Hawaii in 1961. His mother was from America and his father was from Kenya, Africa. Barack's parents divorced while he was still young. After that, Barack's mother married a man from Indonesia. Barack and his mother moved to Indonesia and lived there for a few years. Eventually, he moved back to Hawaii where he went to school at Punahou Academy.

After completing high school, Barack attended a few different colleges, including Occidental College in California, Columbia College in New York, and Harvard Law

School. At Columbia College, Barack studied government and politics, and at Harvard Law School, he studied law. During his time at college, Barack led a few different groups and organizations.

In 1992, Mr. Obama began to teach about the constitution's laws in Chicago, Illinois. Also, in that same year, he married Michelle Robinson, and they had two children together. During her time as **first lady**, Mrs. Obama created programs designed to help children eat healthier.

In 1996, Mr. Obama was elected as an Illinois state senator. He helped to make decisions about Illinois' government. Mr. Obama worked as a state senator until 2004 when he was elected as a Senator in the U.S. Congress.

In 2008, Mr. Obama ran for president as a Democrat and defeated a Republican named John McCain. This is significant in American history because Mr. Obama is the first black man to be elected president.

Immediately, after he was elected, President Obama and the U.S. Congress designed a plan in which American taxpayers' money would be spent in order to help restart the failing economy. However, during his presidency,

America's national debt actually increased more in eight years than in all of the previous presidents' terms combined. It jumped from ten trillion dollars to almost twenty trillion dollars.

During Mr. Obama's presidency, many terrorists did awful things in America and the Middle East. In one instance, in 2012, terrorists attacked the U.S. Consulate in Benghazi, Libya and killed four Americans.

Thankfully, the United States was successful in killing an Islamic terrorist leader named Osama bin Laden. He was the mastermind behind the attacks on America on September 11, 2001. Sadly, though, in April of 2013, shortly after President Obama's second inauguration, two Islamic terrorists bombed the Boston Marathon, killing three Americans and injuring many more. There have also been many other terrorist attacks against Americans since then.

Also, during his presidency, President Obama created a **healthcare** program, called the Affordable Care Act. This program was supposed to help all Americans receive health insurance. However, some parts of the plan did not work the way they were supposed to, and many Americans' healthcare costs actually increased significantly. President Obama's attempt to make healthcare better is known as "Obamacare."

President Obama's terms ended in 2017. He and his family currently live in Washington, D.C.

*Islamic terrorist leader,
Osama bin Laden*

President Obama playing golf

The Obama Family

REVIEW BITES

VOCABULARY

First lady – The wife of a governor or president

Healthcare – Maintenance and improvement of one's health through the use of medical services

FUN FACT

As a teenager, Barack Obama worked at an ice cream shop called Baskin Robbins.

☆☆☆☆☆☆☆☆☆☆☆☆

REVIEW QUESTIONS

1. Where was Barack Obama's father from?

2. Barack Obama was a U.S. Senator from which state?

3. What was President Obama's healthcare program called?

1. Kenya, Africa 2. Illinois 3. "Obamacare"

Donald J. Trump
(2017-Present)

Donald J. Trump

Melania Trump

Donald John Trump was born in New York on June 14, 1946. He was raised in an area called Queensborough in New York City and grew up with four brothers and sisters. Donald went to a school called Kew-Forest and later attended New York Military Academy. While there, Donald became a captain at the academy but never served in the U.S. military.

In 1968, he attended the Wharton School of the University of Pennsylvania and studied economics. While he was in college, Donald worked in his father's company.

In 1971, he took over his father's business and renamed it "The Trump Organization." This was the beginning of Mr. Trump's career as a **businessman.**

In 1973, Mr. Trump began to build many apartments and other buildings called condominiums or **condos.** He has been constructing buildings in America and in many other parts of the world ever since. Mr. Trump has built several large towers across the country, including one in New York City called "Trump Tower." This is where Mr. Trump lived before moving to the White House.

In 1977, Mr. Trump married a woman named Ivana Zelnickova, and they had three children together. However, they divorced in 1991. Mr. Trump then married a woman named Marla Maples, and they had one child together. However, in 1999, they got divorced. In 2005, Mr. Trump married a woman named Melania Knauss, and they had one child together.

In addition to buildings, Mr. Trump has also built golf courses and casinos. Since becoming such a successful businessman, Mr. Trump has acted in movies and even had his own TV show called *The Apprentice.*

Since he owns so many buildings and properties, Mr. Trump has become one of the richest people in America. In 2015, he released papers saying that he was worth over eight billion dollars, which makes him the wealthiest American president.

Mr. Trump has also been interested in politics for many years. He considered running for governor of New York and president many times. In 2000, he decided to run for president but dropped out of the race at the beginning of the primaries. After careful consideration, Mr. Trump ran for president again in 2016 and won.

The election of 2016 was very controversial for both the Democrats and Republicans. Mr. Trump ran as a Republican against Democrat Hillary Clinton, wife of President Bill Clinton. Both sides were accused of lying, cheating, and other scandalous things. However, Mr. Trump won the election, surprising millions of Americans and many in the media, who actually predicted that he would lose by a large margin. At seventy years old, Mr. Trump is the oldest president to ever be elected.

During his campaign, Mr. Trump's slogan was "Make America Great Again." He promised to do many things as president including: improving the U.S. economy by lowering taxes and restoring American jobs, increasing and strengthening the military, building a border wall between the United States and Mexico to help reduce illegal immigration, and repealing President Obama's healthcare plan, called "Obamacare."

Donald Trump's private airplane

Trump Tower in New York City

Donald J. Trump at his presidential inauguration

VOCABULARY

Borough – A town that governs itself

Economics – The study of business and money

Businessman – Someone who owns and runs a business

Condo – An apartment in which a person owns a unit in a multiunit building

FUN FACT

Donald Trump has his own plane called a Boeing 757. While campaigning for president, people called his plane "Trump Force One" because the American president's plane is called "Air Force One."

REVIEW QUESTIONS

1. What did Donald Trump name the business that his father gave him?

2. What is the name of the building in New York City where Donald Trump lived?

3. Whom did Donald Trump defeat in the 2016 presidential election?

1. The Trump Organization 2. Trump Tower
3. Hillary Clinton

Congratulations! You have finished reading <u>U.S. Presidential History Bites!</u>

I hope you have enjoyed it and will continue to learn more about America's history and the presidents.

~Solomon

GLOSSARY

A

Actress – A female actor

Ambassador – Someone who represents a country and visits other nations to tell them about their own country's plans and government

Assemblyman – A man who works in part of a state's government called the Assembly

Attorney – Another word for lawyer; a person who practices law

B

Banking System – A system of banks that takes care of a country's money

Borders – Lines of separation between countries

Borough – A town that governs itself

Brigadier General – A type of leader in the military, who commands a certain number of soldiers

Broadcaster – Someone who announces things on the radio or television

Businessman – Someone who owns and runs a business

Campaign (noun) – An organized effort to get someone elected to a political position

Campaign (verb) – To try and get someone elected for a political office

Capitalism – An economic system that features private ownership of businesses and encourages personal income and profit

Captain – A type of leader in the military, who commands a certain number of soldiers

Career – A job someone keeps for a long time

Case – A legal action or law suit regarding a particular situation

Chief of Staff – A person in charge of a group, organization, or branch of the military

Citizen – A person who is a member of a country

College – A school that people attend when they are older, to learn how to do certain jobs

Colonel – A type of leader in the military, who commands a certain number of soldiers

Colonies – Pieces of land that are ruled by another country

Commissioner – A person in charge of a department or district

Compromise – An agreement that pleases people on both sides of an argument

Condo – An apartment in which a person owns a unit in a multiunit building

Congress – The place where decisions are made concerning America's laws; it is divided into the U.S. Senate and the U.S. House of Representatives

Constitution – A document that explains a country's laws

Constitutional Convention – A place where many important people meet to discuss things about America's Constitution

Convention – A place where many people meet to discuss and decide important things

Coward – Someone who gets easily scared of things

Crime – Things that people do which break the law

Customs – A tax on goods from another country

D

Debates – Discussions and/or arguments between people with differing opinions

Debt – Money that people or a country owe to someone else

Declared war – Announced that there would be a war with another country

Degree – A certificate that is given to someone when they have finished college

Deportation – When a government removes people from its country

Depression – A time when businesses stop running and many people lose their jobs

Devout – Deeply devoted to a religious way of life

Director – A person in charge of an activity, department, or organization

Economics – The study of business and money

Economy – The amount of goods and services a country produces and consumes

Electoral College – A system which gives a person who is running for president a certain number of votes from each state that he/she wins

Electoral Vote – A vote from the electoral college (a voting system for each state and the entire country)

Engineer – Someone who designs machines or buildings

Estate – A big piece of land with a large house

Ferryboat – A boat used to carry people or supplies

Fired – Forced to give up a job

First lady – **The wife of a governor or president**

Foreign policy – **The decisions a government makes about how they are going to deal with other countries**

Funeral – A ceremony that is performed after someone dies

Government – A system that rules a country

Governor – Someone who leads a state or territory

Graduated – When one has completed school and received a diploma (a piece of paper that you get once you finish at a school)

Healthcare – Maintenance and improvement of one's health through the use of medical services

Impeach – To remove a public official from his/her office

Income tax – Money that people have to pay to the government based on how much they earn at their job

In office – Serving in a political job, like the presidency

Issues – Problems or concerns

Judge – Someone who makes decisions in a court based on the law

Landslide – When a person wins an election by a large number of votes

Law firm – A place where people practice law

Law school – A college where someone learns how to be a lawyer

Lawyer – Another word for attorney; a person who practices law

Legislature – A form of government, usually in a city or state

Lieutenant – A type of leader in the military, who commands a certain number of soldiers

Literary – Having to do with reading or literature

Literature – Writings by old or famous authors

Mayor – The leader of a city's government

Military academy – A school that trains military officers

Militia – A separate group of soldiers formed from each state, not part of the military

Minister – A head of a government department who represents their country in other countries

Missiles – Small rockets that can do a lot of damage

National Bank – The system of banking and money for a whole country

National debt – The amount of money that a country has borrowed

National Guard - A group of military reserves of the United States Armed Forces from each state

Navy - An entire force of ships that fight for a country

Negotiating - Trying to arrive at agreements with other people or countries

Nomination - When someone is selected to run for a government office

Opinion - What someone thinks or believes about something

Orphans - Children who do not have any parents

Pardon - To forgive or excuse an error or offense

Plantation - A large farm or estate with resident workers

Pneumonia - A sickness in your lungs that affects your breathing

Political Party – A group of people who believe certain things about how the government should run

Politicians – People who lead a government

Politics – The involvement in a city's, state's, or country's government

Preacher – A man who tells people the truth about the Bible and Jesus Christ during a sermon in church

Private schools – Schools that do not get money from the government and are paid for with tuition

Public Speaker – Someone who speaks in front of a group of people

Public speaking – Speaking in front of a group of people

Purchase – Something that a person buys

R

Ranch – A home on a large piece of land where crops and/or animals are raised

Rebellious – Going against authority and not obeying rules

Reconstruction – The process of bringing the Southern states back into America

Representative – A person who works in a part of the federal government called the House of Representatives

Resigned – Gave up a job

Retirement – The time someone spends once they have finished their life work

Revolution – (This word has two meanings):
      1. A war against a government
      2. A time when things change

Sailors – Men and women who work on ships in a country's navy

Scandal – Something that brings disgrace (embarrassment) to someone famous

Scholarship – When a group or foundation gives a gift of money to someone to help pay for their education

Senator – A person who works in a part of the government called the U.S. Senate

Shoe shiner – Someone who cleans and shines shoes

Speaking tour – A trip on which someone gives speeches

State Senator – A member of a state's senate

Supporters – People who like a person and agree with his or her decisions

Surrendered – Gave up

Surveyor – Someone who measures and records the location of land and buildings

Sworn in – When someone takes an oath and makes a promise to God to be honest and loyal in either what they say, or in their new job

Tailor – Someone who makes and mends people's clothes

Taxes – Money that people have to pay to the government

Tensions – Problems

Term – The time that someone serves as an elected official

Territory – A piece of land that is not a state

Terrorists – People who do things to purposely hurt or scare other people

Tutor – A person who teaches someone else privately

Widow – A woman whose husband has died

Yacht – A large, fancy, and expensive boat